# 2nd Workshop on Linked Data in Linguistics (LDL-2013)



# Representing and Linking Lexicons, Terminologies and Other Language Data

**Collocated with the 6th International Conference on Generative Approaches to the Lexicon**

## Pisa, Italy
## 23 September 2013

**ISBN: 978-1-63266-078-7**

**Printed from e-media with permission by:**

Curran Associates, Inc.
57 Morehouse Lane
Red Hook, NY 12571

CURRAN ASSOCIATES INC.
proceedings.com

**Some format issues inherent in the e-media version may also appear in this print version.**



Printed by Curran Associates, Inc. (2014)



Association for Computational Linguistics
209 N. Eighth Street
Stroudsburg, Pennsylvania 18360

Phone: 1-570-476-8006
Fax: 1-570-476-0860

acl@aclweb.org

**Additional copies of this publication are available from:**

Curran Associates, Inc.
57 Morehouse Lane
Red Hook, NY 12571 USA
Phone: 845-758-0400
Fax: 845-758-2634
Email: curran@proceedings.com
Web: www.proceedings.com

# Table of Contents

# Linguistic Linked Open Data (LLOD)
## Introduction and Overview

*Christian Chiarcos*[1], *Philipp Cimiano*[2], *Thierry Declerck*[3] *& John P. McCrae*[2]

[1] Goethe-Universität Frankfurt am Main, Germany
`chiarcos@uni-frankfurt.de`
[2] Universität Bielefeld, Germany
`{cimiano|jmccrae}@cit-ec.uni-bielefeld.de`
[3] Deutsches Forschungszentrum für Künstliche Intelligenz, Germany
`declerck@dfki.de`

## Abstract

The explosion of information technology has led to a substantial growth in quantity, diversity and complexity of linguistic data accessible over the internet. The lack of interoperability between linguistic and language resources represents a major challenge that needs to be addressed, in particular, if information from different sources is to be combined, like, say, machine-readable lexicons, corpus data and terminology repositories. For these types of resources, domain- specific standards have been proposed, yet, issues of interoperability between different types of resources persist, commonly accepted strategies to distribute, access and integrate their information have yet to be established, and technologies and infrastructures to address both aspects are still under development.
The goal of the 2nd Workshop on Linked Data in Linguistics (LDL-2013) has been to bring together researchers from various fields of linguistics, natural language processing, and information technology to present and discuss principles, case studies, and best practices for representing, publishing and linking linguistic data collections, including corpora, dictionaries, lexical networks, translation memories, thesauri, etc., infrastructures developed on that basis, their use of existing standards, and the publication and distribution policies that were adopted.

## Background: Integrating Information from Different Sources

In recent years, the limited interoperability between linguistic resources has been recognized as a major obstacle for data use and re-use within and across discipline boundaries. After half a century of computational linguistics [8], quantitative typology [12], empirical, corpus-based study of language [10], and computational lexicography [16], researchers in computational linguistics, natural language processing (NLP) or information technology, as well as in Digital Humanities, are confronted with an immense wealth of linguistic resources, that are not only growing in number, but also in their heterogeneity.

Interoperability involves two aspects [14]:

**Structural ('syntactic') interoperability:** Resources use comparable formalisms to represent and to access data (formats, protocols, query languages, etc.), so that they can be accessed in a uniform way and that their information can be integrated with each other.

**Conceptual ('semantic') interoperability:** Resources share a common vocabulary, so that linguistic information from one resource can be resolved against information from another resource, e.g., grammatical descriptions can be linked to a terminology repository.

With the rise of the Semantic Web, new representation formalisms and novel technologies have become available, and different communities are becoming increasingly aware of the potential of these developments with respect to the challenges posited by the heterogeneity and multitude of linguistic resources available today. Many of these approaches follow the **Linked (Open) Data paradigm** [1] that postulates four rules for the publication and representation of Web resources: (1) Referred entities should be designated by using URIs, (2) these URIs should be resolvable over HTTP, (3) data should be represented by means of W3C standards (such as RDF), (4) and a resource should include links to other resources. These rules facilitate information integration, and thus, interoperability, in that they require that entities can be addressed in a globally unambiguous way (1), that they can be accessed (2) and interpreted (3), and that entities that are associated on a conceptual level are also physically associated with each other (4).

In the definition of Linked Data, the **Resource Description Framework (RDF)** receives special attention. RDF was designed to provide metadata about resources that are available either offline (e.g., books in a library) or online (e.g., eBooks in a store). RDF provides a generic data model based on labeled directed graphs, which can be serialized in different formats. Information is expressed in terms of *triples* - consisting of a *property* (relation, i.e., a labeled edge) that connects a *subject* (a resource, i.e., a labeled node) with its *object* (another resource, or a literal, e.g., a string). RDF resources (nodes)[1] are represented by *Uniform Resource Identifiers (URIs).* They are thus globally unambiguous in the web of data. This allows resources hosted at different locations to refer to each other, and thereby to create a network of data collections whose elements are densely interwoven.

Several data base implementations for RDF data are available, and these can be accessed using **SPARQL** [17], a standardized query language for RDF data. SPARQL uses a triple notation similar to RDF, only that properties and RDF resources can be replaced by variables. SPARQL is inspired by SQL, variables can be introduced in a separate `SELECT` block, and constraints on these variables are expressed in a `WHERE` block in a triple notation. SPARQL does not only support running queries against individual RDF data bases that are accessible over HTTP (so-called 'SPARQL end points'), but also, it allows us to combine information from multiple repositories (federation). RDF can thus not only be used to *establish* a network, or cloud, of data collections, but also, to *query* this network directly.

[1]The term 'resource' is ambiguous: *Linguistic* resources are structured collections of data which can be represented, for example, in RDF. In RDF, however, 'resource' is the conventional name of a node in the graph, because, historically, these nodes were meant to represent objects that are described by metadata. We use the terms 'node' or 'concept' whenever *RDF* resources are meant in ambiguous cases.

RDF has been applied for various purposes beyond its original field of application. In particular, it evolved into a generic format for knowledge representation. RDF was originally conceived as the building block of the **Semantic Web** and was then readily adopted by disciplines as different as biomedicine and bibliography. Due to its application across discipline boundaries, RDF is maintained by a large and active community of users and developers, and it comes with a rich infrastructure of APIs, tools, databases, query languages, and multiple sub-languages that have been developed to define data structures that are more specialized than the graphs represented by RDF. These sub-languages can be used to create *reserved vocabularies* and *structural constraints* for RDF data. For example, the Web Ontology Language (OWL) defines the datatypes necessary for the representation of ontologies as an extension of RDF, i.e., *classes* (concepts), *instances* (individuals) and *properties* (relations).

The concept of Linked Data is closely coupled with the idea of **openness** (otherwise, the linking is only partially reproducible), and in 2010, the original definition of Linked Open Data has been extended with a 5 star rating system for data on the Web.[2] The first star is achieved by publishing data on the Web (in any format) under an open license, and the second, third and fourth star require machine-readable data, a non-proprietary format, and using standards like RDF, respectively. The fifth star is achieved by linking the data to other people's data to provide context. If (linguistic) resources are published in accordance with these rules, it is possible to follow links between existing resources to find other, related data and exploit network effects.

## Linked Data: Benefits

Publishing Linked Data allows resources to be globally and uniquely identified such that they can be retrieved through standard Web protocols. Moreover, resources can be easily linked to one another in a uniform fashion and thus become structurally interoperable. Linking to central terminology repositories facilitates conceptual interoperability. Beyond this, Chiarcos et al. [7] identified the following main benefits of Linked Linguistic Data: (a) linking through URIs, (b) federation, (c) dynamic linking between resources, and (d) the availability of a rich ecosystem of formats and technologies.

### Linking through URIs

Linked Data requires that every resource is identified by a Uniform Resource Identifier (URI) that figures both as a global identifier and as a Web address – i.e., a description of the resource is available if you request it from its URI on the Web. However, RDF allows for a standard description of such resources on the Web and hence for automatic processing of these resources. It is not necessarily the case that the data must be solely available as RDF, as the HTTP protocol supports *content negotiation*: as one example, the RDF data under `http://de.dbpedia.org/data/Linked_Open_Data.rdf` can be rendered in human-readable HTML, see `http://de.dbpedia.org/page/Linked_Open_Data`.

[2] `http://www.w3.org/DesignIssues/LinkedData.html`, paragraph 'Is your Linked Open Data 5 Star?'

### Information Integration at Query Runtime (Federation)

As resources can be uniquely identified and easily referenced from any other resource on the Web through URIs, the connections between these resources can be navigated even during query runtime. In effect, this allows the creation of a linked web of data similar to the effect of hyperlinks in the HTML Web. Moreover, it is possible to use existing Semantic Web methods such as Semantic PingBack [18] to be informed of new incoming links to your resource. Along with HTTP-accessible repositories and resolvable URIs, it is possible to combine information from physically separated repositories in a single query at runtime. Information from different resources in the cloud can then be integrated freely.

### Dynamic Import

If cross-references between linguistic resources are represented by resolvable URIs instead of system-defined ID references or static copies of parts from another resource, it is not only possible to resolve them at runtime, but also to have access to the most recent version of a resource. For community-maintained terminology repositories like the ISO TC37/SC4 Data Category Registry [20, 19, ISOcat], for example, new categories, definitions or examples can be introduced occasionally, and this information is available immediately to anyone whose resources refer to ISOcat URIs.

### Ecosystem

RDF as a data exchange framework is maintained by an interdisciplinary, large and active community, and it comes with a developed infrastructure that provides APIs, database implementations, technical support and validators for various RDF-based languages, e.g., reasoners for OWL. For developers of linguistic resources, this ecosystem can provide technological support or off-the-shelf implementations for common problems, e.g., the development of a database that is capable of supporting flexible, graph-based data structures as necessary for multi-layer corpora [15].

Beyond this, another advantage warrants a mention: The distributed approach of the Linked Data paradigm facilitates the distributed development of a web of resources and collaboration between researchers that provide and use this data and that employ a shared set of technologies. One consequence is the emergence of interdisciplinary efforts to create large and interconnected sets of resources in linguistics and beyond. LDL-2013 aims to provide a forum to discuss and to facilitate such on-going developments.

## LLOD: Building the Cloud

Recent years have seen not only a number of approaches to provide linguistic data as Linked Data, but also the emergence of larger initiatives that aim at interconnecting these resources, culminating in the creation of a Linguistic Linked Open Data (LLOD) cloud, i.e., a Linked Open Data (sub-)cloud of linguistic resources.

LDL-2013 is organized in the context of two recent community efforts, the Open Linguistics Working Group (OWLG), and the W3C Ontology-Lexica Community Group (OntoLex). The Open Linguistics Working Group has spearheaded the creation of new data and the republishing of existing linguistic resources as part of the emerging Linguistic Linked Open Data (LLOD) cloud. Similarly, the W3C Ontology-Lexica Community Group is seeking to develop standard models for representing and publishing (ontology-) lexica and other lexical resources as RDF.

## The LLOD Cloud

Aside from benefits arising from the actual *linking* of linguistic resources, various linguistic resources from various fields have been provided in RDF and related standards in the last decade.

In particular, this is the case for **lexical resources** (Fig. 1, LEXICON), e.g., WordNet [11], which represent a cornerstone of the Semantic Web and which are firmly integrated in the Linked Open Data (LOD) cloud. Other types of linguistic resources with less relevance for AI and Knowledge Representation, however, have been absent from the LOD cloud.

The Linked Data paradigm also facilitates the management of information about language (Fig. 1, LANGUAGE_DESCRIPTION), i.e., linguistic terminology and linguistic databases. **Terminology repositories** serve an important role to establish conceptual interoperability between language resources. If resource-specific annotations or abbreviations are expanded into references to repositories of linguistic terminology and/or metadata categories, linguistic annotations, grammatical features and metadata specifications become more easily comparable. Important repositories developed by different communities include GOLD [9] and ISOcat [20, 19], yet, only recently these terminology repositories were put in relation with each other using Linked Data principles and with linguistic resources, e.g., within the OLiA architecture [5]. **Linguistic databases** are a particularly heterogeneous group of linguistic resources; they contain complex and manifold types of information, e.g., feature structures that represent typologically relevant phenomena, along with examples for their illustration and annotations (glosses) and translations applied to these examples (structurally comparable to corpus data), or word lists (structurally comparable to lexical-semantic resources). RDF as a generic representation formalism is thus particularly appealing for this class of resources.

Finally, for **linguistic corpora** (Fig. 1, CORPORA), the potential of the Linked Data paradigm for modeling, processing and querying of corpora is immense, and RDF conversions of semantically annotated corpora have been proposed early [3]. RDF provides a graph-based data model as required for the interoperable representation of arbitrary kinds of annotation [2, 15], and this flexibility makes it a promising candidate for a general means of representation for corpora with complex and heterogeneous annotations. RDF does not only establish interoperability between annotations within a corpus, but also between corpora and other linguistic resources [4]. In comparison to other types of linguistic resources, corpora are currently underrepresented in the LLOD cloud, but the development of schemes for corpora and/or NLP annotations represents an active line of research [6, 13] also addressed in the workshop.

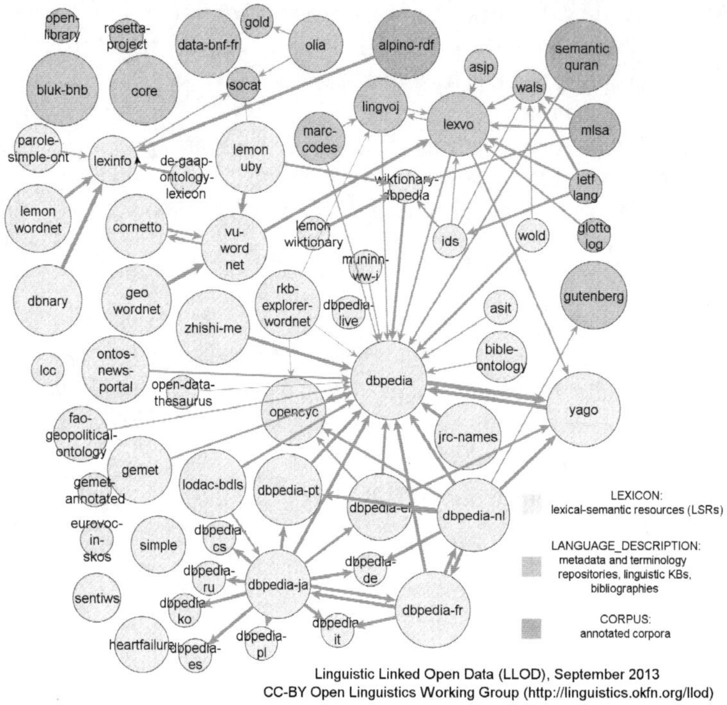


Figure 1: Linguistic Linked Open Data cloud as of September 2013.

Only recently, the efforts to apply RDF to linguistic resources of different types have begun to converge towards an actual Linked Open Data (sub-) cloud of linguistic resources, the Linguistic Linked Open Data (LLOD) cloud.

## Community Efforts

The LLOD cloud is a result of a coordinated effort of the **Open Linguistics Working Group (OWLG)**,[3] a network open to anyone interested in linguistic resources and/or the publication of these under an open license. The OWLG is a working group of the Open Knowledge Foundation (OKFN),[4] a community-based non-profit organization promoting open knowledge (i.e., data and content that is free to use, re-use and to be distributed without restriction).

Since its formation in 2010, the Open Linguistics Working Group has grown steadily. One of our primary goals is to attain openness in linguistics through:

1. Promoting the idea of open linguistic resources,
2. Developing the means for the representation of open data, and
3. Encouraging the exchange of ideas across different disciplines.

[3]`http://linguistics.okfn.org`
[4]`http://okfn.org/`

The OWLG represents an open forum for interested individuals to address these and related issues. At the time of writing, the group consists of about 100 people from 20 different countries. Our group is relatively small, but continuously growing and sufficiently heterogeneous. It includes people from library science, typology, historical linguistics, cognitive science, computational linguistics, and information technology; the ground for fruitful interdisciplinary discussions has been laid out. One concrete result emerging out of collaborations between a large number of OWLG members is the LLOD cloud as already sketched above.

The emergence of the LLOD cloud out of a set of isolated resources was accompanied and facilitated by a series of **workshops and publications** organized under the umbrella of the OWLG, including the Open Linguistics track at the Open Knowledge Conference (OKCon-2010, July 2010, Berlin, Germany), the First Workshop on Linked Data in Linguistics (LDL-2012, March 2012, Frankfurt am Main, Germany), the Workshop on Multilingual Linked Open Data for Enterprises (MLODE-2012, September 2012, Leipzig, Germany), the Linked Data for Linguistic Typology track at ALT-2012 (September 2013, Leipzig, Germany). Plans to create a LLOD cloud were first publicly announced at LDL-2012, and subsequently, a first instance of the LLOD materialized as a result of the MLODE-2012 workshop, its accompanying hackathon and the data postproceedings that will appear as a special issue of the Semantic Web Journal (SWJ). The Second Workshop on Linked Data in Linguistics (LDL-2013) continues this series of workshops. In order to further contribute to the integration of the field, it is organized as a joint event of the OWLG and the W3C Ontology-Lexica Community Group.

The **Ontology-Lexica Community (OntoLex) Group**[5] was founded in September 2011 as a W3C Community and Business Group. It aims to produce specifications for a lexicon-ontology model that can be used to provide rich linguistic grounding for domain ontologies. Rich linguistic grounding includes the representation of morphological, syntactic properties of lexical entries as well as the syntax-semantics interface, i.e., the meaning of these lexical entries with respect to the ontology in question. An important issue herein will be to clarify how extant lexical and language resources can be leveraged and reused for this purpose. As a byproduct of this work on specifying a lexicon-ontology model, it is hoped that such a model can become the basis for a web of lexical linked data: a network of lexical and terminological resources that are linked according to the Linked Data Principles forming a large network of lexico-syntactic knowledge.

The OntoLex W3C Community Group has been working for more than a year on realizing a proposal for a standard ontology lexicon model, currently discussed under the the designation *lemon*. As the core specification of the model is almost complete, the group started to develop of additional modules for specific tasks and use cases, and some of these are presented at LDL-2013.

# LDL-2013: The 2nd Workshop on Linked Data in Linguistics

The goal of the 2nd Workshop on Linked Data in Linguistics (LDL-2013) has been to bring together researchers from various fields of linguistics, NLP,

[5] `http://www.w3.org/community/ontolex`

and information technology to present and discuss principles, case studies, and best practices for representing, publishing and linking linguistic data collections, including corpora, dictionaries, lexical networks, translation memories, thesauri, etc., infrastructures developed on that basis, their use of existing standards, and the publication and distribution policies that were adopted.

For the 2nd edition of the workshop on Linked Data in Linguistics, we invited contributions discussing the application of the Linked Open Data paradigm to linguistic data as it might provide an important step towards making linguistic data: i) easily and uniformly queryable, ii) interoperable and iii) sharable over the Web using open standards such as the HTTP protocol and the RDF data model. Recent research in this direction has lead to the emergence of a Linked Open Data cloud of linguistic resources, the Linguistic Linked Open Data (LLOD) cloud, where Linked Data principles have been applied to language resources, allowing them to be published and linked in a principled way. Although not restricted to lexical resources, these play a particularly prominent role in this context. The topics of interest mentioned in the call for papers were the following ones:

1. Use cases for creation, maintenance and publication of linguistic data collections that are linked with other resources
2. Modelling linguistic data and metadata with OWL and/or RDF
3. Ontologies for linguistic data and metadata collections
4. Applications of such data, other ontologies or linked data from any subdiscipline of linguistics
5. Descriptions of data sets, ideally following Linked Data principles
6. Legal and social aspects of Linguistic Linked Open Data

In response to our call for papers we received 17 submissions which were all reviewed by at least two members of our program committee. On the basis of these reviews, we decided to accept 8 papers as full papers and 2 as short papers, giving an overall acceptance rate of around 50%.

LDL-2013 was collocated with the 6th International Conference on Generative Approaches to the Lexicon (GL2013): Generative Lexicon and Distributional Semantics, and hence, **lexical-semantic resources** represent a particularly important group of resources at the current edition of the workshop.

The contributions by Koide and Takeda and Bartolini et al. describe the conversion of the Japanese and Italian WordNet and related resources as well as their linking to (L)LOD resources such as the DBpedia.

Buitelaar et al. describe the specification and use of a model for the interoperable representation of language resources for sentiment analysis. The model is based directly on *lemon*, and in the EuroSentiment project it will be used to represent language resources for sentiment analysis such as WordNet Affect in a interoperable way.

Similarly, Moran and Brümmer employ *lemon* for the modeling of dictionary and wordlist data made available by a project on quantitative historical linguistics. Using Linked Data principles, more than fifty disparate lexicons and dictionaries were combined into a single dataset, which then provides researchers with a translation graph allowing users to query across the underlying lexicons and dictionaries to extract semantically-aligned wordlists.

An extension of *lemon* is developed by Fiorelli et al. who present LIME (Linguistic Metadata), a new vocabulary aiming at completing *lemon* with specifications for linguistic metadata. In many usage scenarios currently developed as extensions of *lemon* (e.g. ontology alignment, localization etc...), the discovery and exploitation of linguistically grounded datasets may benefit from reassuming information about their linguistic expressivity. While the VoID vocabulary covers the need for general metadata about linked datasets, specifically linguistic information demands a dedicated extension.

Finally, Bonial et al. describe SemLink, a comprehensive resource for NLP that maps and unifies several high quality lexical resources: PropBank, VerbNet, FrameNet, and OntoNotes sense groupings. Each of these resources was created for different purposes, and therefore each carries unique strengths and limitations. SemLink allows users to leverage the strengths of each resource and provides the groundwork for incorporating these lexical resources effectively. Although SemLink is not immediately based on the application of the Linked Data paradigma, it represents an important contribution to the LLOD cloud, as it provides links between classical resources for word-level semantics (e.g., WordNet) long established in the (L)LOD cloud, and frame-semantic resources. In this function, an earlier instantiation of SemLink represents a fundamental component of the lemonUby data set shown in Fig. 1.

An approach to model of **language description** data as Linked Data is presented by Littauer et al. who feed spreadsheet data about a group of endangered languages and where they are spoken in West Africa into an RDF triple store. They use RDF tools to organize and visualize these data on a world map, accessible through a web browser. The functionality they develop allows researchers to see where these languages are spoken and to query the language data, thereby providing a powerful tool for linguists studying the genealogical relatedness of the Dogon languages.

A different type of information about language is addressed by Hayashi who describes the modeling of psycholinguistic semantic feature norms. Semantic feature norms, originally utilized in the field of psycholinguistics as a tool for studying human semantic representation and computation, have recently attracted some NLP/IR researchers who wish to improve their task performances. Currently available semantic feature norms are, however, rarely well structured, making them difficult to integrate with existing resources of various types. This paper provides a case study, it extracts a tentative set of semantic feature norms that are psycholinguistically considerable, and draws a technical map to formalize them by observing the Linked Data paradigm.

LDL-2013 features three contributions addressing **corpora** that we identified above as being underrepresented in the LLOD cloud: Menke et al. describe a framework for releasing multimodal corpora as Linked Data, and experiences in releasing a multimodal corpus based on an online chat game on that basis. Heuss presents an experiment in translating excerpts of a natural language story into a formal RDF structure, so that it is accessible by machines on a word or concept level. Finally, Pareja-Lora et al. describe the first steps taken to transform a set of linguistic resources from the Data Transcription and Analysis Tool's (DTA) metadata and data into an open and interoperable language resource.

## Acknowledgements

We would like to express our gratitude to the organizers of the GL2013 for hosting our workshop and support with respect to local organization. Further, we thank the OWLG and its members for active contributions to the LLOD cloud, to the workshop and beyond. In particular, we have to thank the contributors and the program committee for their invaluable work and engagement.

## Bibliography

[1] T. Berners-Lee. Design issues: Linked data. URL `http://www.w3.org/DesignIssues/LinkedData.html` (July 31, 2012), 2006.

[2] S. Bird and M. Liberman. A formal framework for linguistic annotation. *Speech Communication*, 33(1-2):23–60, 2001.

[3] A. Burchardt, S. Padó, D. Spohr, A. Frank, and U. Heid. Formalising multi-layer corpora in OWL/DL – lexicon modelling, querying and consistency control. In *3rd International Joint Conference on NLP (IJCNLP 2008)*, Hyderabad, India, 2008.

[4] C. Chiarcos. Interoperability of corpora and annotations. In C. Chiarcos, S. Nordhoff, and S. Hellmann, editors, *Linked Data in Linguistics*, pages 161–179. Springer, Heidelberg, 2012.

[5] C. Chiarcos. Ontologies of linguistic annotation: Survey and perspectives. In *8th International Conference on Language Resources and Evaluation (LREC-2012)*, pages 303–310, Istanbul, Turkey, May 2012.

[6] C. Chiarcos. POWLA: Modeling linguistic corpora in OWL/DL. In *9th Extended Semantic Web Conference (ESWC-2012)*, pages 225–239, Heraklion, Crete, May 2012.

[7] C. Chiarcos, J. McCrae, P. Cimiano, and C. Fellbaum. Towards open data for linguistics: Linguistic linked data. In A. Oltramari, Lu-Qin, P. Vossen, and E. Hovy, editors, *New Trends of Research in Ontologies and Lexical Resources*. Springer, Heidelberg, to appear.

[8] L. Dostert. The Georgetown-IBM experiment. In W. Locke and A. Booth, editors, *Machine Translation of Languages*, pages 124–135. John Wiley & Sons, New York, 1955.

[9] S. Farrar and T. Langendoen. Markup and the GOLD ontology. In *EMELD Workshop on Digitizing and Annotating Text and Field Recordings*. Michigan State University, July 2003.

[10] W. N. Francis and H. Kucera. Brown Corpus manual. Technical report, Brown University, Providence, Rhode Island, 1964. revised edition 1979.

[11] A. Gangemi, R. Navigli, and P. Velardi. The OntoWordNet project: Extension and axiomatization of conceptual relations in WordNet. In R. Meersman and Z. Tari, editors, *Proceedings of On the Move to Meaningful Internet Systems (OTM2003)*, pages 820–838, Catania, Italy, November 2003.

[12] J. Greenberg. A quantitative approach to the morphological typology of languages. *International Journal of American Linguistics*, 26:178–194, 1960.

[13] S. Hellmann, J. Lehmann, and S. Auer. Linked-data aware URI schemes for referencing text fragments. In *18th International Conference on Knowledge Engineering and Knowledge Management (EKAW-2012)*, Galway, Ireland, 2012.

[14] N. Ide and J. Pustejovsky. What does interoperability mean, anyway? Toward an operational definition of interoperability. In *Second International Conference on Global Interoperability for Language Resources (ICGL 2010)*, Hong Kong, China, 2010.

[15] N. Ide and K. Suderman. GrAF: A graph-based format for linguistic annotations. In *1st Linguistic Annotation Workshop (LAW 2007)*, pages 1–8, Prague, Czech Republic, 2007.

[16] W. Morris, editor. *The American Heritage Dictionary of the English Language*. Houghton Mifflin, New York, 1969.

[17] E. Prud'Hommeaux and A. Seaborne. SPARQL query language for RDF. *W3C working draft*, 4(January), 2008.

[18] S. Tramp, P. Frischmuth, N. Arndt, T. Ermilov, and S. Auer. Weaving a distributed, semantic social network for mobile users. In *8th Extended Semantic Web Conference (ESWC-2011)*, pages 200–214, Heraklion, Crete, 2011.

[19] M. Windhouwer and S.E. Wright. Linking to linguistic data categories in ISOcat. In C. Chiarcos, S. Nordhoff, and S. Hellmann, editors, *Linked Data in Linguistics*, pages 99–107. Springer, Heidelberg, 2012.

[20] S.E. Wright. A global data category registry for interoperable language resources. In *Proceedings of the Fourth Language Resources and Evaluation Conference (LREC 2004)*, pages 123–126, Lisboa, Portugal, May 2004.

## Organizing Committee

| | |
|---|---|
| Christian Chiarcos | Johan Wolfgang Goethe Universität Frankfurt |
| Philipp Cimiano | Universität Bielefeld |
| Thierry Declerck | Deutsches Forschungszentrum für Künstliche Intelligenz |
| John Philip McCrae | Universität Bielefeld |

## Program Committee

| | |
|---|---|
| Guadalupe Aguado | Universidad Politécnica de Madrid, Spain |
| Maria Blume | Cornell University, USA |
| Peter Bouda | Interdisciplinary Centre for Social and Language Documentation, Portugal |
| Steve Cassidy | Macquarie University, Australia |
| Damir Cavar | Eastern Michigan University, USA |
| Michael Cysouw | Ludwig-Maximilian-Universität München, Germany |
| Ernesto William De Luca | University of Applied Sciences Potsdam, Germany |
| Gerard de Melo | University of California at Berkeley, USA |
| Dongpo Deng | Institute of Information Sciences, Academia Sinica, Taiwan |
| Alexis Dimitriadis | Universiteit Utrecht, The Netherlands |
| Judith Eckle-Kohler | Technische Universität Darmstadt, Germany |
| Jeff Good | University at Buffalo, USA |
| Jorge Gracia | Universidad Politécnica de Madrid, Spain |
| Harald Hammarström | Radboud Universiteit Nijmegen, The Netherlands |
| Yoshihiko Hayashi | Osaka University, Japan |
| Sebastian Hellmann | Universität Leipzig, Germany |
| Dominic Jones | Trinity College Dublin, Ireland |
| Lutz Maicher | Universität Leipzig, Germany |
| Pablo Mendes | Open Knowledge Foundation Deutschland, German |
| Elena Monsiel-Ponsoda | Universidad Politécnica de Madrid, Spain |
| Steven Moran | Universität Zürich, Switzerland/Ludwig Maximilian University, Germany |
| Sebastian Nordhoff | Max Planck Institute for Evolutionary Anthropology, Leipzig, Germany |
| Antonio Pareja-Lora | Universidad Complutense Madrid, Spain |
| Felix Sasaki | Deutsches Forschungszentrum für Künstliche Intelligenz, Germany |
| Andrea Schalley | Griffith University, Australia |
| Marieke van Erp | VU University Amsterdam, The Netherlands |
| Menzo Windhouwer | Max Planck Institute for Psycholinguistics, Nijmegen, The Netherlands |
| Alena Witzlack-Makarevich | Universität Zürich, Switzerland |

# Linguistic Linked Data for Sentiment Analysis

**Paul Buitelaar, Mihael Arcan**
DERI, Unit for NLP,
National University of Ireland, Galway
{paul.buitelaar, mihael.arcan}@deri.org

**Carlos A. Iglesias, J. Fernando Sánchez-Rada**
Dept. Ing. Sist. Telemáticos,
Univ. Politécnica de Madrid,
Spain
{cif, jfernando}@gsi.dit.upm.es

**Carlo Strapparava**
Human Language Technology
FBK, Italy
strappa@fbk.eu

## 1 Introduction

In this paper we describe the specification of a model for the semantically interoperable representation of language resources for sentiment analysis. The model integrates 'lemon', an RDF-based model for the specification of ontology-lexica (Buitelaar et al. 2009), which is used increasingly for the representation of language resources as Linked Data, with 'Marl', an RDF-based model for the representation of sentiment annotations (Westerski et al., 2011; Sánchez-Rada et al., 2013).

In the EuroSentiment project, the lemon/Marl model will be used to represent lexical resources for sentiment and emotion analysis such as SentiWordNet (Baccianella et al. 2010) and WordNet Affect[1] (Strapparava and Valitutti 2004), as well as other language resources such as sentiment annotated corpora, in a semantically interoperable way, using Linked data principles.

The representation of WordNet resources in lemon depends on a straightforward conversion of the WordNet data model, but importantly we introduce the use of URIs to uniquely and formally define structure and content of this WordNet based language resource. URIs are adopted from existing Linked Data resources, thereby further enhancing semantic interoperability. We further integrate a notion of domains into this representation in order to enable domain-specific definition of polarity for each lexical item.

The lemon model allows for the representation of all aspects of lexical information, including lexical sense (word meaning) and polarity, but also morphosyntactic features such as part-of-speech, inflection, etc. This kind of information is not provided by WordNet Affect but will be available from other language resources, including those available at EuroSentiment partners that can be easily integrated with the WordNet Affect information using lemon.

The representation of sentiment polarity uses concepts from Marl.

## 2 Motivation

Sentiment analysis is now an established field of research and a growing industry (Po et al. 2008). However, language resources for sentiment analysis are being developed by individual companies or research organisations and are normally not shared, with the exception of a few publicly available resources such as WordNet Affect and SentiWordNet. Domain-specific resources for multiple languages are potentially valuable but not shared, sometimes due to IP and licence considerations, but often because of technical reasons, including interoperability.

In the EuroSentiment project we envision instead a pool of semantically interoperable language resources for sentiment analysis, including domain-specific lexicons and annotated corpora. Sentiment analysis applications will be able to: access domain-specific polarity scores for individual lexical items in the context of semantically defined sentiment lexicons and corpora, or access and integrate complete language resources. Access may be restricted according to commercial considerations, with payment schedules in place, or may be partially free. A semantic service access layer will be put in place for this purpose.

## 3 The lemon Model

The lexicon model for ontologies (lemon) builds on previous work on standards for the representation of lexical resources, i.e., the Lexical Markup Framework (LMF[2]) but extends the underlying formal model and provides a native integration of lexica with domain ontologies. The lemon model is

[1] http://wndomains.fbk.eu/wnaffect.html

[2] http://www.lexicalmarkupframework.org/

described in detail in the lemon cookbook (McCrae et al. 2010). Here we provide a summary of its most prominent features, starting with the lemon core, which is organized around a core path as follows:

- *Ontology Entity*: URI of an ontology element to which a Lexical Form points, providing a possible linguistic realisation for that Ontology Entity
- *Lexical Sense*: functional object that links a Lexical Entry to an Ontology Entity, providing a sense-disambiguated interpretation of that Lexical Entry
- *Lexical Entry*: morpho-syntactic normalisation of one or more Lexical Form
- *Lexical Form*: morpho-syntactic variant of a Lexical Entry, including inflection, declination and syntactic variation
- *Representation*: standard written or phonetic representation for a Lexical Form

In addition, lemon has a number of modules that allow for further modelling. Currently defined modules are: linguistic description, phrase structure, morphology, syntax and mapping, variation. *The linguistic description module* is concerned with the use of ISOcat data categories for describing lemon elements. Although lemon itself is a meta-model and therefore agnostic as regards the specific data category set used, we use a specific set of data categories in particular instances of the lemon model, such as LexInfo (Cimiano et al. 2011).

*The phrase structure module* is concerned with the modelling of lexical entries that are syntactically complex, such as phrases and clauses. The module provides tokenisation and phrase structure analysis to enable representation of the syntactic structure of such lexical entries.

*The morphology module* is concerned with the analysis and representation of inflectional and agglutinative morphology. The module allows the specification of regular inflections of words by use of Perl-like regular expressions, which greatly simplifies the creation of lexical entries for highly synthetic and inflectional languages.

*The syntax and mapping module* is concerned with a description of lexical 'predicates' (subcategorisation frames with syntactic arguments) and semantic predicates (properties with subject/object) on the ontology side and the mapping between them. The module allows a mapping to be specified as a one-to-one correspondence.

*The variation module* is concerned with a description of the relationships between the elements of a lemon lexicon, which are split into three classes: sense relations, lexical variations, form variations. Sense relations require a semantic context, such as translation. Lexical variations require a morphosyntactic context, such as plural. Form variations are all other variations, such as homographs.

An interesting aspect of lemon-based ontology lexicalisation is the use of URIs for uniquely identifying all objects defined by the lemon model (lexicons, lexical entries, words, phrases, forms, variants, senses, references, etc.), which can be linked and maintained in a flexible, modular and distributed way. The lemon model can therefore contribute significantly to the development of Lexical Linked Data (McCrae et al. 2011, Nuzzolese et al. 2011, McCrae et al. 2012), which in turn will greatly enhance distributed development, exchange, maintenance and use of lexical resources as well as of ontologies as they will be increasingly tightly integrated with lexical knowledge.

In the context of the EuroSentiment project we will exploit the lemon model exactly for this purpose: representing language resources for sentiment analysis in a Linked Data conform way (RDF-native form), enabling leverage of existing Semantic Web technologies (SPARQL, OWL, RIF etc.).

## 4 The Marl Sentiment Ontology

Marl is an ontology for annotating sentiment expressions, which will be used by the EuroSentiment service layer to describe the output of sentiment analysis services as well as by the resource layer to describe the sentiment properties of lexical entries. For this latter purpose in particular, the Marl ontology is used in combination with lemon as illustrated above.

The Marl ontology is a vocabulary designed for annotation and description of subjective opinions expressed in text. The goals of the Marl ontology are to:

- enable publishing raw data about opinions and the sentiments expressed in them
- deliver schema that will allow to compare opinions coming from different systems (polarity, topics and features)

• interconnect opinions by linking them to contextual information expressed from other popular ontologies or specialised domain ontologies.

The Marl ontology has been extended according to the needs of the EuroSentiment project. In particular, the main extension has been its alignment with the PROV-O Ontology (Lebo, 2013) in order to support provenance modelling. The PROV-O ontology is part of the PROV Family (Groth, 2012; Gil, 2012) that provides support for modelling and interchange of provenance on the Web and Information Systems.

Provenance is information about entities, activities and people involved in producing a piece of data or thing, which can be used to form assessment about its quality, reliability and trustworthiness. The main concepts of PROV are entities, activities and agents. Entities are physical or digital assets, such as web pages, spell checkers or, in our case, dictionaries or analysis services. Provenance records describe the provenance of entities, and an entity's provenance can refer to other entities. For example, a dictionary is an entity whose provenance refers to other entities such as lexical entries. Activities are how entities come into existence. For example, starting from a web page, a sentiment analysis activity creates an opinion entity describing the extracted opinions from that web page. Finally, agents are responsible for the activities and can be a person, a piece of software, an organisation or other entities. The Marl ontology has been aligned with the PROV ontology so that provenance of language resources can be tracked and shared.

Sentiment Analysis is an Activity that analyses a Source text according to an algorithm and produces an opinion about the entities described in the source text. The main features of the extracted opinion are the polarity (positive, neutral or negative), the polarity value or strength whose range is defined between a min and max value, and the described entity and feature of that opinion. Opinions can also be aggregated opinions of a set of users.

For a better understanding of the ontology itself, we present below the main classes and properties that form the ontology:

• *Opinion*: a subclass of the Provenance Entity that represents the results of a Sentiment Analysis process. Among its classes we find:

• *describesObject*: property that points to the object the opinion refers to.

• *describesObjectPart*: optional property, used whenever the opinion specifies the part of the object it refers to, not only the general object.

• *describesObjectFeature*: aspect of the object or part that the user is giving an opinion of.

• *hasPolarity*: polarity of the opinion itself, to be chosen from the available Opinion individuals.

• *polarityValue*: degree of the polarity. In other words, it represents how strong the opinion (independently of the polarity) is.

• *algorithmConfidence*: rating the analysis algorithm has given to this particular result. Can be interpreted as the accuracy or trustworthiness of the information

• *extractedFrom*: original source text or resource from which the opinion was extracted.

• *opinionText*: part of the source that was used in the sentiment analysis. That is, the part of the source that contained sentiment information.

• *domain*: context domain of the result. The same source can be analysed in different domains, which would lead to different results.

• *AggregatedOpinion*: when several opinions are equivalent, we can opt to aggregate them into an "AggregatedOpinion", which in addition to the properties we already covered, it presents these properties:

• *opinionCount*: the number of individual opinions this AggregatedOpinion represents.

• *Polarity*: base class to represent the polarity of the opinion. In every opinion, we will use an instance of this class. The base Marl ontology comes with three instances: Positive, Negative, Neutral

• *SentimentAnalysis*: in Marl, the process of sentiment analysis is also represented semantically, which allows us to understand the opinion data, trace it and keep several results by different algorithms, linking all of them to the process that created them. The main properties of each SentimentAnalysis class are: minPolarityValue: lower limit for polarity values in the opinions extracted via this analysis activity; maxPolarityValue: upper limit for polarity values in the opinions extracted via this analysis activity.

• *Algorithm*: algorithm that was used in the analysis. Useful to group opinions by extraction algorithm and compare them.

• *source*: site or source from which the opinion was extracted. There are two reasons behind this property: grouping by opinion source (e.g. opinions from IMDB) and treating and interpreting opinions from the same source in the same manner.

An example application of the Marl ontology for a sentiment analysis service is shown in the Appendix. It is split in two: a view of the representation of the analysis (Fig 1), and a representation of the result (Fig 2).

## 5 Representation of WordNet Affect

In this section we describe how language resources based on the Princeton WordNet model (Miller 1995) such as WordNet Affect can be represented using lemon.

WordNet Affect is an extension of the WordNet database, including a subset of synsets suitable to represent affective concepts. Similarly to the extension related to domain labels, one or more affective labels (a-labels) are assigned to a number of WordNet synsets. In particular, the affective concepts representing emotional state are individuated by synsets marked with the a-label 'emotion'. The emotional categories are hierarchically organized in order to specialize synsets with a-label emotion and to distinguish synsets according to emotional valence. There are also other a-labels for concepts representing moods, situations eliciting emotions, or emotional responses[3].

Unique and independently established URIs for WordNet synsets allow for a distributed representation that enable Semantic Web based linking between and integration of WordNet based as well as other language resources. We illustrate this here with an example from WordNet Affect, using English based WordNet 3.0 URIs as defined by the Europeana project.

Consider the following example for the English noun 'fear' in WordNet and equivalent Italian synonyms taken from the Italian WordNet (i.e. this holds for any English aligned Wordnet) in WordNet Affect:

**Princeton WordNet:**

*n#05590260 12 n 03 fear 0 fearfulness 0 fright 0 017 @ 05560878 n 0000 ! 05595229 n 0101 = 00080744 a 0000 = 00084648 a 0000 ~ 05590744 n 0000 ~ 05590900 n 0000 ~ 05591021 n 0000 ~ 05591212 n 0000 ~ 05591290 n 0000 ~ 05591377 n 0000 ~ 05591481 n 0000 ~ 05591591 n 0000 ~ 05591681 n 0000 ~ 05591792 n 0000 ~ 05592739 n 0000 ~ 05593389 n 0000 %p 10337259 n 0000 | an emotion experienced in anticipation of some specific pain or danger (usually accompanied by a desire to flee or fight)*

**WordNet Affect:**

*n#05590260 fifa paura spavento terrore timore | "una emozione che si prova prima di qualche specifico dolore o pericolo"*
*n#05590260 affective-label="negative-fear"*
*n#05590260 domain-label="Psychological_Features"*

***lemon* transformation & integration:**

Using lemon we can represent and integrate information on the Italian synonyms, their links to the English based synset using Princeton WordNet URIs, and sentiment properties using Marl. Domain properties will be based on WordNet Domains[4]. The example illustrates the positive polarity of 'fear' in English (and 'fifa, paura, spavento, terrore' in Italian) in the context of 'horror movies' and negative polarity in the context of 'children movies'.

Declaration of namespaces used – *wn* declares WordNet 3.0 synsets, *lemon* declares the core lemon lexicon model, *lexinfo* declares specific properties for part-of-speech etc., *wd* declares domain categories, *marl* declares sentiment properties:

*@prefix wn: <http://semanticweb.cs.vu.nl/europeana/lod/purl/vocabularies/princeton/wn30/> .*
*@prefix lemon: <http://www.monnet-project.eu/lemon#> .*
*@prefix lexinfo: <http://www.lexinfo.net/ontology/2.0/lexinfo#> .*
*@prefix wd: <http://www.eurosentiment.eu/wndomains/> .*
*@prefix marl: <http://purl.org/marl/ns#> .*

Declaration of lexicon identifier, language and lexical entries:

```
:lexicon a lemon:Lexicon ;
  lemon:language "it" ;
  lemon:entry   :fifa,
                :paura,
                :spavento,
                :terrore.
```

[3] A SKOS version of WordNet Affect is available from http://gsi.dit.upm.es/ontologies/wnaffect/

[4] http://wndomains.fbk.eu/

Declaration of lemma, sense (link to synset in WordNet 3.0, polarity and domain context) and part-of-speech of 'fifa':

```
:fifa a lemon:Lexicalentry ;
 lemon:canonicalForm [ lemon:writtenRep
"fifa"@it ] ;
 lemon:sense [ lemon:reference wn:synset-fear-noun-1;
          marl:polarityValue 0.375 ;
          marl:hasPolarity marl:positive ;
          lemon:context wd:horror_movies ] ;
 lemon:sense [ lemon:reference wn:synset-fear-noun-1;
          marl:polarityValue 0.375 ;
          marl:hasPolarity marl:negative ;
          lemon:context wd:children_movies ];
 lexinfo:partOfSpeech lexinfo:noun .
```

Declarations of lemma and part-of-speech of 'paura, spavento, terrore, timore':

```
:paura a lemon:Lexicalentry ;
  lemon:canonicalForm [ lemon:writtenRep
          "paura"@it ] ;
  lexinfo:partOfSpeech lexinfo:noun .

:spavento a lemon:Lexicalentry ;
  lemon:canonicalForm [ lemon:writtenRep
          "spavento"@it ] ;
  lexinfo:partOfSpeech lexinfo:noun .

:terrore a lemon:Lexicalentry ;
  lemon:canonicalForm [ lemon:writtenRep
          "terrore"@it ] ;
  lexinfo:partOfSpeech lexinfo:noun .

:timore a lemon:Lexicalentry ;
  lemon:canonicalForm [ lemon:writtenRep
          "timore"@it ] ;
  lexinfo:partOfSpeech lexinfo:noun .
```

Declarations of sense equivalence (synonymy) of 'paura, spavento, terrore, timore' with 'fifa':

```
:paura a lemon:LexicalSense ;
          lemon:equivalent :fifa.

:spavento a lemon:LexicalSense ;
          lemon:equivalent :fifa.

:terrore a lemon:LexicalSense ;
          lemon:equivalent :fifa.

:timore a lemon:LexicalSense ;
          lemon:equivalent :fifa..
```

## 6 Representation of Lexical and Sentiment Features

The examples discussed in the previous section showed the representation of WordNet based language resources with lemon. However also many other types of language resources exist, including sentiment dictionaries maintained by the EuroSentiment use case partners that define domain words with their polarity scores as well as inflectional variants, part-of-speech, etc. We can also represent such language resources using lemon combined with Marl, thereby making them interoperable with the lemon version of WordNet Affect as well as other lemon based language resources.

Consider the following example for the German noun 'Einschlag' ('impact') with lexical features (inflection, part-of-speech) and polarity score:

```
Einschlag    Einschlag NN negative -/-0.0048/- L
Einschlages  Einschlag NN negative -/-0.0048/- L
Einschlags   Einschlag NN negative -/-0.0048/- L
Einschläge   Einschlag NN negative -/-0.0048/- L
Einschlägen  Einschlag NN negative -/-0.0048/- L
```

Using lemon and Marl we can represent this and integrate it with additional information as follows:

Declaration of namespaces used – *wn* declares WordNet 3.0 synsets, *lemon* declares the core lemon lexicon model, *isocat* declares specific properties for part-of-speech etc. (*isocat* is part of the *lexinfo* model used in the previous example), *marl* declares sentiment properties:

```
@prefix wn:
<http://semanticweb.cs.vu.nl/europeana/lod/purl/vo-
cabularies/princeton/wn30/> .
@prefix lemon: <http://www.monnet-
project.eu/lemon#> .
@prefix isocat: <https://catalog.clarin.eu/isocat/inter-
face/index.html> .
@prefix marl:
<http://gsi.dit.upm.es/ontologies/marl/ns#> .
```

Declaration of lexicon identifier, language and lexical entry:

```
:lexicon a lemon:Lexicon ;
  lemon:language "de" ;
  lemon:entry :Einschlag.
```

Declaration of lemma, sense (link to synset in WordNet 3.0, polarity), alternate forms (inflectional variants with features), part-of-speech and sentiment polarity:

```
:Einschlag
```

```
lemon:canonicalForm [
  lemon:writtenRep "Einschlag"@de ;
      isocat:DC-1297 isocat:DC-1883 ;
      # gender=masculine
      isocat:DC-1298 isocat:DC-1387 ;
      # number=singular
      isocat:DC-2720 isocat:DC-1331 ] ;
      # case=nominative
  lemon:sense [ lemon:reference
      wn:synset-impact-noun-1;
      marl:polarityValue 0.0048;
       marl:hasPolarity marl:negative ] ;
  lemon:altForm
    [ lemon:writtenRep "Einschlages"@de ;
      isocat:DC-1297 isocat:DC-1883 ;
      # gender=masculine
      isocat:DC-1298 isocat:DC-1387 ;
      # number=singular
      isocat:DC-2720 isocat:DC-1293 ] ;
      # case=genitive
    [ lemon:writtenRep "Einschlags"@de ;
      isocat:DC-1297 isocat:DC-1883 ;
      # gender=masculine
      isocat:DC-1298 isocat:DC-1387 ;
      # number=singular
      isocat:DC-2720 isocat:DC-1293 ] ;
      # case=genitive
   [ lemon:writtenRep "Einschläge"@de ;
      isocat:DC-1297 isocat:DC-1883 ;
      # gender=masculine
      isocat:DC-1298 isocat:DC-1354 ;
      # number=plural
      isocat:DC-2720 isocat:DC-1331 ] ;
      # case=nominative
   [ lemon:writtenRep "Einschlägen"@de ;
      isocat:DC-1297 isocat:DC-1883 ;
      # gender=masculine
      isocat:DC-1298 isocat:DC-1354 ;
      # number=plural
      isocat:DC-2720 isocat:DC-1265 ] ;
      # case=dative
isocat:DC-1345 isocat:DC-1333.
# partOfSpeech=noun.
```

## 7 Ongoing and Future Work

Sentiment Analysis aims at determining the attitude of the writer to some topic (positive, negative, neutral). Emotion analysis goes one step further and aims at determining the emotional or affective state of the writer when writing. In EuroSentiment, we have defined two vocabularies for annotating sentiment and emotion expressions, called Marl and Onyx, respectively. In this paper we focused on the representation of sentiment annotations with Marl. The definition and representation of emotion expressions with Onyx is ongoing work, with the objective of covering different theoretical models of emotions (Sánchez-Rada et al., 2013). Onyx will support the representation and use of several emotion taxonomies such as WordNet Affect or EmotionML

Our ongoing and future work is concerned also with the definition and implementation of a work flow that will enable the generation of domain-specific semantically interoperable lexica for sentiment analysis. The work flow will use lemon and Marl for the representation and integration of:

- WordNet Domains information on domain(s)
- domain entity information from DBpedia and/or other relevant semantic resources
- WordNet Affect information on synsets (using Onyx)
- morphosyntactic information (part-of-speech, inflection, ...) from other language resources in the EuroSentiment Language Resource Pool
- SentiWordNet scores and/or automatically extracted domain sentiment scores

Given a particular sentiment analysis task domain, the approach is based on the analysis of a representative text collection for the purpose of entity identification, synset disambiguation, morphosyntactic analysis, and domain-specific polarity value extraction.

## 8 Conclusions

We presented a model for the specification, integration and use of language resources for sentiment analysis based on Linked Data principles.

The presented model is based directly on the lemon and Marl ontologies for the representation of Linked Data based lexical resources and sentiment expressions respectively. This work is now being extended so that emotion analysis is also addressed.

In the context of the EuroSentiment project the combined model will be used for the integrated and semantically interoperable representation of sentiment dictionaries and annotations. As a result, EuroSentiment will make available lexical resources based on this interoperable representation with the aim of fostering the development of services using sentiment analysis.

## Acknowledgments

This work was partially funded by the EC for the FP7 project EuroSentiment under Grant Agreement 296277 and in part by a research grant from Science Foundation Ireland (SFI) under Grant Number SFI/12/RC/2289 for the INSIGHT project.


## References


Baccianella, Stefano, Andrea Esuli and Fabrizio Sebastiani, "SENTIWORDNET 3.0: An Enhanced Lexical Re-source for Sentiment Analysis and Opinion Mining", Proc. of LREC, 2010.

Buitelaar, Paul, Philipp Cimiano, Peter Haase, and Michael Sintek. "Towards linguistically grounded ontologies." In The Semantic Web: Research and Applications, pp. 111-125. Springer Berlin Heidelberg, 2009.

Cimiano, Philipp, Paul Buitelaar, John McCrae, and Michael Sintek. "LexInfo: A declarative model for the lexicon-ontology interface." Web Semantics: Science, Services and Agents on the World Wide Web 9, no. 1 (2011): 29-51.

Ekman, Paul. "Basic emotions." Handbook of cognition and emotion 98 (1999): 45-60.

Gil, Yolanda and Simon Miles, "PROV Model Primer", W3C Working Draft, 11th December 2012, available at http://www.w3.org/TR/2012/WD-prov-primer-20121211/.

Groth, Paul and Luc Moreau, "PROV Overview", W3C Working Draft, 11th December 2012, available at http://www.w3.org/TR/2012/WD-prov-overview-20121211/.

Lebo, Timothy, Satya Sahoo and Deborah McGuinness, "PROV-O: The PROV Ontology", W3C Recommendation, 30th April 2013, available at http://www.w3.org/TR/prov-o/, 2013.

McCrae, John, Guadalupe Aguado-de-Cea, Paul Buitelaar, Philipp Cimiano, Thierry Declerck, Asunción Gómez-Pérez, Jorge Gracia et al. "Interchanging lexical resources on the semantic web." Language Resources and Evaluation 46, no. 4 (2012): 701-719.

McCrae, John, Dennis Spohr, and Philipp Cimiano. "Linking lexical resources and ontologies on the semantic web with lemon." In The Semantic Web: Research and Applications, pp. 245-259. Springer Berlin Heidelberg, 2011.

McCrae, John, Guadalupe Aguado-de-Cea, Paul Buitelaar, Philipp Cimiano, Thierry Declerck, Asunción Gómez Pérez, Jorge Gracia et al. "The lemon cookbook." (2010).

Miller, George A. "WordNet: a lexical database for English." Communications of the ACM 38.11 (1995): 39-41.

Nuzzolese A, Gangemi A, Presutti V (2011) Gathering lexical linked data and knowledge patterns from framenet. In: Proceedings of the sixth international conference on Knowledge capture, ACM, pp 41–48.

Pang, Bo and Lee, Lillian, "Opinion mining and sentiment analysis" Foundations and trends in information retrieval, 2008.

Prinz, Jesse. Gut Reactions: A Perceptual Theory of Emotion (Oxford: Oxford University Press, 2004): page 157

Sánchez-Rada, J. Fernando, Onyx Ontology Specification, V1.2 July 2013, available at http://www.gsi.dit.upm.es/ontologies/onyx/

Strapparava, Carlo, and Alessandro Valitutti. "WordNet-Affect: an affective extension of WordNet." In Proceedings of LREC, vol. 4, pp. 1083-1086. 2004.

Westerski, Adam, Carlos A. Iglesias and Fernando Tapia, "Linked Opinions: Describing Sentiments on the Structured Web of Data." In Proceedings of the 4th International Workshop Social Data on the Web, 2011.

Westerski, Adam and Sánchez-Rada, J. Fernando, Marl Ontology Specification, V1.0 May 2013, available at http://www.gsi.dit.upm.es/ontologies/marl/

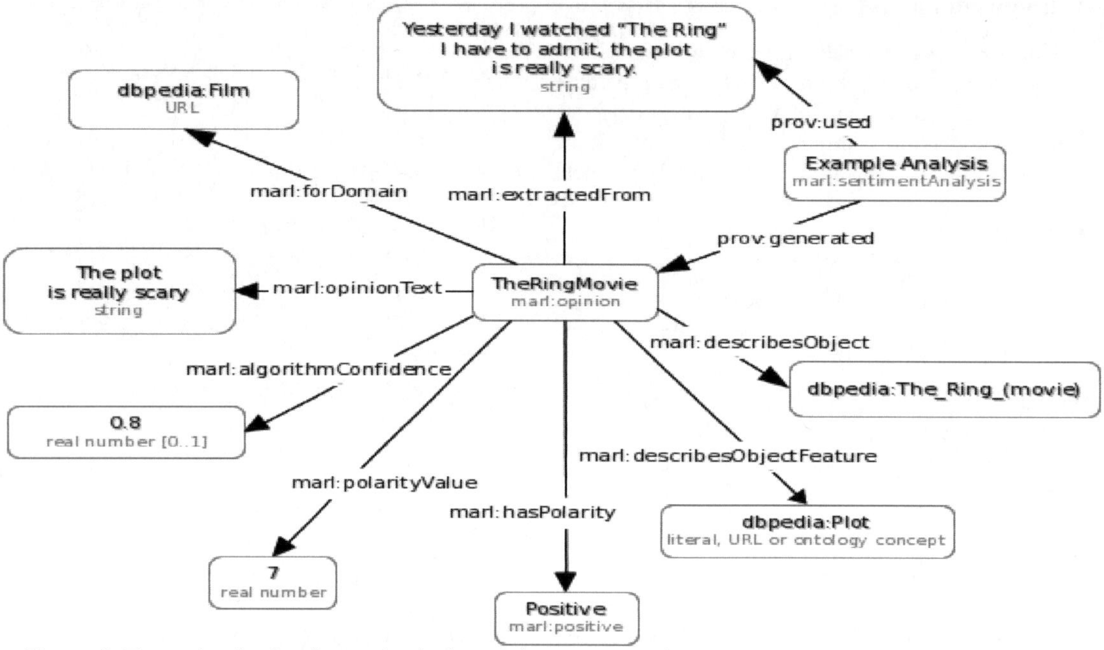

Figure 1: Example of a Sentiment Analysis activity representation

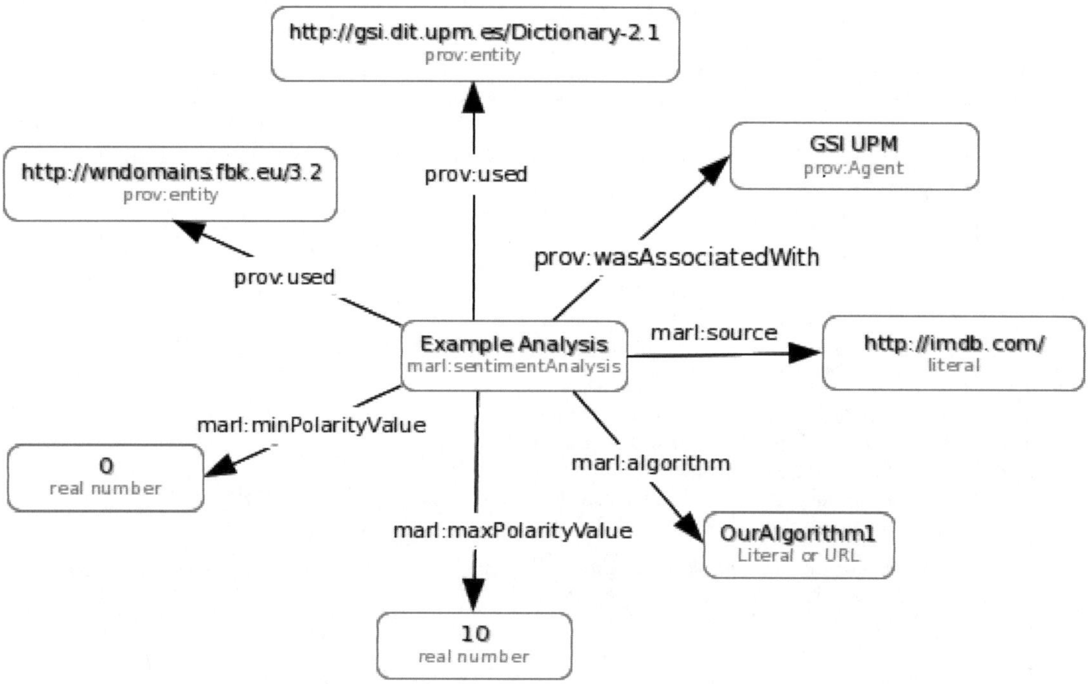

Figure 2: Example Sentiment Analysis result

# Renewing and Revising SemLink

**Claire Bonial, Kevin Stowe & Martha Palmer**
Department of Linguistics,
University of Colorado at Boulder
Hellems 290, 295 UCB
Boulder, CO 80309-0295
{Claire.Bonial, Kevin.Stowe, Martha.Palmer}@colorado.edu

## Abstract

This research describes SemLink, a comprehensive resource for Natural Language Processing that maps and unifies several high-quality lexical resources: PropBank, VerbNet, FrameNet, and the recently added OntoNotes sense groupings. Each of these resources was created for slightly different purposes, and therefore each carries unique strengths and limitations. SemLink allows users to leverage the strengths of each resource and provides the groundwork for incorporating these lexical resources effectively into linked data resources. SemLink and the resources included therein are discussed with a focus on the value of using lexical resources in a complementary fashion. Recent improvements to SemLink, including the addition of a new resource, the OntoNotes sense groupings, are described. Work to address future goals, including further expansion of SemLink, is also discussed.

## 1 Introduction

SemLink (Palmer, 2009) is an ongoing effort to map complementary lexical resources: PropBank (PB) (Palmer et al., 2005), VerbNet (VN) (Kipper et al., 2008), FrameNet (FN) (Fillmore et al., 2002), and the recently added OntoNotes (ON) sense groupings (Pradhan et al., 2007). Each of these lexical resources varies in the level and nature of semantic detail represented, since each was created independently with somewhat differing goals. Nonetheless, all of these resources can be used to associate semantic information with the propositions of natural language. SemLink serves as a platform to unify these resources and therefore combine the fine-granularity and rich semantics of FN, the syntactically-based generalizations of VN, and the relatively coarse-grained semantics of PB, which has been shown to be effective training data for supervised Machine Learning techniques. The recent addition of ON sense groupings, which can be thought of as a more semantically general view of WordNet (Fellbaum, 1998), provides even broader coverage for the resource.

Although SemLink has been created independently from Semantic Web technology, it is in an important tool for integrating the resources therein into linked data lexical resources, such as *lemonUby* (Eckle-Kohler, McCrae and Chiarcos, submitted). Semlink provides a single link to a lexical unit, which can then access all of these resources at once. For linked data in linguistics to be leveraged effectively, it is necessary to have systems that can automatically recognize that, for example, 'Stock prices *decreased*' and 'The stock market is *falling*' describe the same event. Such an interpretation relies upon a recognition of the similarity between *decrease* and *fall*, as well as between *stock prices* and *stock market*. This requires rich lexical resources that make these connections explicit. While WordNet and FN alone contribute much towards this goal, much more needs to be done to appropriately interpret polysemous verbs in context. SemLink helps to address this need.

SemLink unifies the aforementioned lexical resources by firstly providing a mapping between the semantic roles of PB and VN, as well as a mapping between the semantic roles of VN and the Frame Elements of FN. Each of these resources differ primarily in the granularity, or level of semantic specificity, of the semantic roles used. For example, PB uses very generic labels such as Arg0, as in:

[Arg0 President Bush] has [REL approved] [Arg1 duty-free treatment for imports of certain types of watches.]

In addition to providing several alternative syntactic frames and a set of semantic predicates corresponding to verbs within a class, VN marks the PB Arg0 as an Agent, and the Arg1 as a Theme, using traditional thematic role labels. In contrast, FN labels them as Grantor and Action respectively, and puts them in the Grant Permission class, thereby situating the event within a certain semantic domain or frame. The additional semantic richness provided by VN and FN does not contradict PB, but can be seen as complementary. It should also be noted that while the explicit numbered argument label itself within PB is quite generic, PB also includes a lexical resource where these numbered arguments are further specified, and these descriptions are verb-specific and therefore quite fine-grained.

SemLink provides an additional level of unification by providing a mapping between the verb senses, or 'rolesets' of PB and VN classes, and in turn between VN classes and FN frames. Like the semantic roles, these senses also differ in their levels of granularity. For example, the verb *hear* has just one coarse-grained sense in PB, with the following roleset:

**Arg0**: hearer
**Arg1**: utterance, sound
**Arg2**: speaker, source of sound

This sense maps to both the Discover and See classes of VN, and the Perception_Experience and Hear frames of FN. Each resource provides a unique lexicon, again varying in the extent to which verb senses are either lumped together or distinguished. SemLink helps to leverage the contributions of each component, as well as take advantage of manual annotations created for each resource.

## 2 The Resources Included in SemLink

As discussed initially, the resources described here are distinct but complementary to each other. The question is, how can we best leverage the contributions of each one in a broad-coverage English lexical resource? In the quest for more annotated data and, in particular more diverse genres, it would clearly be advantageous to be able to take the manual data annotations that have been created with respect to one resource and merge them with data annotations for other resources. This could create a much larger, more diverse and yet still coherent training corpus; this is one of the goals of the SemLink project. This section provides background on each individual resource.

### 2.1 PropBank

Unlike FN and VN, the primary goal in developing the Proposition Bank, or PB, was not lexical resource creation, but the development of an annotated corpus to be used as training data for supervised machine learning systems. The first PB release consists of 1M words of the Wall Street Journal portion of the Penn Treebank II (Marcus & Marcinkiewicz, 1993) with predicate-argument structures for verbs, using semantic role labels for each verb argument. Although the semantic role labels are purposely chosen to be quite generic and theory neutral, Arg0, Arg1, etc., they are still intended to consistently annotate the same semantic role across syntactic variations (Arg0 and Arg1 do consistently correspond to Dowty's (1991) concepts of Proto-Agent and Proto-Patient respectively). For example, the Arg1 or Patient in 'John broke the window' is the same window that is annotated as the Arg1 in 'The window broke,' even though it is the syntactic subject in one sentence and the syntactic object in the other. Thus, the main goal of PB is to supply consistent, simple, general purpose labeling of semantic roles for a large quantity of coherent text to support the training of automatic semantic role labelers, in the same way the Penn Treebank has supported the training of statistical syntactic parsers.

As mentioned previously, PB also provides a lexicon entry for each broad meaning of every annotated verb, including the possible arguments of the predicate and their labels (its 'roleset') and all possible syntactic realizations. For example, the verb *leave* includes the following two rolesets, which correspond to syntactically and semantically distinct senses of the verb:

**Roleset ID**: leave.01 *move away from*
**Roles**:
Arg0: entity leaving
Arg1: place, person, or thing left
Arg2: attribute of arg1
Example: *John left Mary alone.*

**Roleset ID**: leave.02 *give*
**Roles**:
Arg0: giver/leaver
Arg1: thing given

Arg2: benefactive, given-to
Example: *Mary left her daughter the diamond pendant.*

This lexical resource is used as a set of verb-specific guidelines by the annotators, and can be seen as quite similar in nature to FN and VN although at a more coarse-grained level. In addition to numbered roles, PB defines several more general (ArgM, Argument Modifier) roles that can apply to any verb, and which are similar to adjuncts. These include LOCation, EXTent, ADVerbial, CAUse, TeMPoral, MaNneR, and DIRection, among others. These are marked, for example, as 'ArgM-LOC.'

In spite of its success in facilitating the training of semantic role labeling (SRL), there are several ways in which PB could be more effective. PB lacks much of the information that is contained in VN, including information about selectional restrictions, verb semantics, and inter-verb relationships. We have therefore created the mapping between VN and PB included in SemLink, which will allow us to use the machine learning techniques that have been developed for PB annotations to generate VN representations.

The mapping between VN and PB consists of two parts: a lexical mapping and an annotated corpus. The lexical mapping is responsible for specifying the potential mappings between PB and VN for a given word; but it does not specify which of those mappings (typically one to many) should be used for any given occurrence of the word. That is the job of the annotated corpus, which for any given instance gives the specific VN mapping and semantic role labels. This can be thought of as a form of sense tagging: where a PB frame maps to several VN classes, they can be thought of as more fine-grained senses, and labeling with the class label corresponds to providing a sense tag label.

The type-to-type lexical mapping was used to automatically predict VN classes and role labels for each instance. Where the resulting mapping was one-to-many, the correct mapping was selected manually (Loper et al., 2007). The usefulness of this mapping for improving SRL on new genres has been demonstrated by Yi, Loper, and Palmer (2007) who focused on Arg2 . By subdividing the Arg2 instances into coherent subgroups based on the VN labels and then using them for training, and then mapping back to Arg2 for testing, the performance on Arg2 increased 6 points for WSJ test data, and 10 points for Brown Corpus test data. These results encouraged extending the mappings to other resources, starting with FN.

### 2.2 VerbNet

VN is midway between PB and FN in terms of lexical specificity, and is closer to PB in its close ties to syntactic structure. It consists of hierarchically arranged verb classes, inspired by and extended from Levin's verb classes (Levin, 1993). The original Levin classes constitute the first few levels in the hierarchy, with each class subsequently refined to account for further semantic and syntactic differences within a class. In many cases, the additional information that VN provides for each class has caused it to subdivide, or use intersections of, Levin classes. Each class and subclass is characterized extensionally by its set of verbs, and intensionally by a list of the arguments of those verbs and syntactic and semantic information about them. Subclasses add information about behaviors and characteristics shared by a subset of verbs in the class.

In each class and subclass, an effort is made to list all syntactic frames in which the verbs of that class can be grammatically realized. Each syntactic frame is detailed with the expected syntactic phrase type of each argument, thematic roles of arguments, and a semantic representation; for example:

**Frame** NP V NP PP.destination
**Example** Jessica loaded boxes into the wagon.
**Syntax** Agent V Theme Destination
**Semantics** Motion(during(E), Theme)
Not(Prep-*into*(start(E), Theme, Destination))
Prep-*into*(end(E), Theme, Destination)
Cause(Agent, E)

Although this classification is primarily based on shared syntactic behaviors, there is clear semantic cohesion to each of the classes. As Levin hypothesizes, this is a result of the fact that verb behavior is a reflection of verb meaning.

### 2.3 FrameNet

Based on Fillmore's Frame Semantics, each semantic frame in FN is defined with respect to its Frame Elements, which are fine-grained semantic role labels. For instance, the Frame Elements for the Apply-heat Frame include a Cook, Food and a Heating Instrument. More traditional labels for the same roles might be Agent, Theme and Instrument. Members of the Apply-heat frame include *bake, barbecue, blanch, boil, braise, broil, brown,* etc. The Apply-heat lexical units all happen to be verbs, but a frame can also have adjectives and nouns as members.

The 1,033 lexical frames are associated with over 10,000 Frame Elements, since there is a deliberate effort to keep the Frame Element names distinct whenever there are semantic differences (Fillmore et al., 2002). The Frame Elements for an individual Frame are classified in terms of how central they are, with three levels being distinguished: core (similar to syntactically obligatory), peripheral (similar to syntactically optional), and extrathematic (similar to adjuncts rather than arguments). Lexical items are grouped together based solely on having the same frame semantics, without consideration of similarity of syntactic behavior, unlike Levin's verb classes. Sets of verbs with similar syntactic behavior may appear in multiple frames, and a single FN frame may contain sets of verbs with related senses but different subcategorization properties. FN places a primary emphasis on providing rich, idiosyncratic descriptions of semantic properties of lexical units in context, and making explicit subtle differences in meaning.

The SemLink VN/FN mapping consists of three parts. The first part is a many-to-many mapping of VN Classes and FN frames for specific class members. It is many-to-many in that a given FN lexical unit can map to more than one VN member, and more frequently, a given VN member can map to more than one FN Frame. The second part is a mapping of VN semantic roles and FN frame elements. These two parts have been provided in separate files in order to offer the cleanest possible formatting. The third part is the PB corpus with mappings from PB roleset ID's to FN frames and mappings from the PB arguments to FN frame elements. This has recently been manually updated and corrected due to changes in each resource; this process is discussed in more detail in 3.1.

### 2.4 OntoNotes Sense Groupings

The ON Sense Groupings can be thought of as a more coarse-grained view of WordNet senses. This is because these sense groupings were based on WordNet senses that were successively merged into more coarse-grained senses based on the results of inter-annotator agreement in tagging of the senses (Duffield et al., 2007; Pradhan et al., 2007). Essentially, where two annotators were consistently able to distinguish between two senses, the distinction was kept. Where annotators were not able to consistently distinguish between two senses, the senses were conflated into one sense. For example, the sense groupings for the verb *leave* include the following 6 senses, whereas the WordNet entry includes 14 senses:

**Sense 1** name='depart, go forth, exit'
**Sense 2** name='leave something behind...'
**Sense 3** name='cause an effect that remains'
**Sense 4** name='stop, terminate, end'
**Sense 5** name='exclude, neglect to include'
**Sense 6** name='end a romantic relationship'

These groupings also include recently updated, manually created links to WordNet senses, VN classes and PB Framesets. Because the SemLink portion of the Wall Street Journal has also been annotated with these sense groupings, the annotation portion of SemLink has recently been augmented with the appropriate sense grouping for each instance, therefore providing an additional mapping level to the SemLink corpus. The incorporation of ON sense groupings into SemLink is discussed in more detail in 3.2.

## 3 Current State of SemLink

The first version of SemLink (1.1) contained mappings between the three lexical resources discussed (PB, VN, and FN), as well as a collection of predicates from the Wall Street Journal data annotated with PB and VN classes and arguments. In the recent release (SemLink 1.2, available for download here: http://verbs.colorado.edu/semlink/), these WSJ propositions have been additionally annotated with FN frames and FN frame elements (using FN version 1.5), as well as ON sense groupings. The mapping files between PB, VN (version 3.2), and FN have also been checked for consistency and updated to more accurately reflect the current relations between these resources.

### 3.1 FN Addition to Corpus

The first major improvement made to SemLink is the addition of FN frames and FN frame elements to the corpus annotation. SemLink 1.1 contained mappings from VN classes to FN frames (e.g. Remove-10.1 to Change_of_leadership for class member *depose*), as well as mappings from VN thematic roles to FN frame elements (e.g. Agent to Selector for Change_of_leadership frame), but contained no FN information for specific Wall Street Journal predicates within the corpus. The current SemLink version contains manually annotated FN frames for most of these WSJ propositions, as well as automatic mappings where this was possible because the existing mapping was one-to-one. Additionally, the VN thematic role to FN frame element mapping file was used to populate the arguments for each proposition. Thus, the SemLink corpus now contains PB argument information, VN thematic roles, and the appropriately mapped FN frame elements.

The addition of FN information to the corpus data allows for a detailed inspection of these various lexical resources in language practice. The mapping files of SemLink 1.1 allowed for an overview of the granularity differences between these resources, but applying all three of them to the corpus data gives a clear picture of how each resource handles various argument structures, as well as how the resources interact and overlap with each other. With the corpus data thus annotated, a verb can be examined to see how it behaves with regard to each resource, as well as how these resources interact across a corpus.

### 3.2 Addition of OntoNotes Senses to SemLink

To improve and expand the variety of resources mapped by SemLink, ON sense grouping annotations were added to the corpus data in the latest SemLink release. As mentioned previously, the ON senses are derived from the WordNet sense groupings, but are more coarse-grained and allow for better inter-annotator agreement. Sense distinctions with this level of granularity can be detected automatically at 87-89% accuracy, making them effective for NLP applications (Dligach and Palmer, 2011). The coverage of ON annotations isn't complete - only 37,389 of approximately 80,000 have this annotation (although surely some of these are monosemous verbs). The current annotation covers all verbs with more than three senses and is therefore quite useful despite its incomplete coverage, but further annotation is necessary to complete the mapping of this resource.

### 3.3 Updates & Corrections

A pressing challenge for the SemLink project is keeping the resources that it maps properly aligned. The three major lexical resources undergo frequent revisions to improve accuracy and coverage, and the mappings between them subsequently require updates and improvements. SemLink 1.2 contains a large amount of manual updates between the mappings as well as improvements to the processes used to keep these resources aligned in the future.

The VN to FN mapping files are incredibly useful but are also challenging. Maintaining the accuracy and completeness of the files is particularly difficult, as neither resource maintains an explicit connection to the other. The mapping files between these resources were originally created and curated by hand, so that as these resources have been updated, the mapping files fall out of date. The development of SemLink 1.2 required an implementation of error checking in these files, which would indicate which VN classes, FN frames, VN thematic roles, and FN frame elements were no longer present. This allowed for these files to be checked for explicit errors and brought up to date with the current releases of both resources.

The mapping file between VN and PB contained similar errors, as both PB and VN are frequently revised, but a long-term solution for correcting these discrepancies has been developed. PB contains within its framesets explicit, hand-annotated mappings between PB frames and VN classes. The VN to PB mapping file was generated from these annotations, giving a current, accurate version of the mappings between these two resources.

With the updates to all three resources and their mapping files, the Wall Street Journal predicates were also found to contain errors resulting from antiquated annotations. Approximately one third of the instances from the original VN to PB WSJ mappings in the original SemLink contained mappings that are no longer valid, or incorrect annotations as VN and PB have been updated. The current implementation of SemLink checks each PB roleset and VN class against the current data and mapping files, and marks it for reannotation if there are any discrepancies. In this way, the WSJ data is kept consistent with the mapping files and the current versions of each resource.

## 4 Leveraging SemLink

Natural Language Processing applications vary widely in their of use of resources, and different applications require different levels of granularity. Research in automatic semantic role labeling has demonstrated the importance of the level of granularity of semantic roles: Yi, Loper and Palmer (2007) and Loper et al. (2007) both demonstrate that because VN labels are more generalizable across verbs than PB labels, they are easier for semantic role labeling systems to learn; however, Merlo and Van Der Plas (2009) found that the differing levels of granularity of PB and VN were both useful, and therefore suggest complementary use of both resources.

SemLink attemps to bring together both coarse and fine-grained resources and make them easily useable and interchangable. If an application requires a fine-grained resource like FN, but the available data is annotated only with a coarse-grained resource like PB, SemLink provides a bridge to make that data useable. As the coverage of SemLink expands to more data, more lexical units, and more resources, this functionality becomes more and more useful in traversing the gap between different annotations and different resource-oriented goals. Efforts to expand and improve SemLink and some of the individual resources therein are discussed in the sections to follow.

The utility of integrating resources generally, and of SemLink in particular, is also reflected in the work on UBY (Eckle-Kohler et al., 2012; Gurevychy et al., 2012), a large scale lexical semantic resource using lexical markup framework (an ISO-standard for modeling lexical resources) to uniformly represent and combine a wide range of lexical-semantic resources, like WordNet, FN and VN, but also Wiktionary and Wikipedia in both English and German. This project made use of SemLink's mappings between VN classes and FN frames to supplement its integration of resources. The UBY project brings to light the need to expand such mappings to resources between many languages, instead of being limited to English. Ideally, SemLink could in the future integrate with or expand into such a multilingual resource, for instance by linking Arabic or Hindi PropBank rolesets.

Most recently, UBY has been converted into RDF using the *lemon* lexicon model (McCrae et al., 2012; Eckle-Kohler, McCrae and Chiarcos, submitted), to create *lemonUby*. *lemon* is a lexicon model that has been specifically developed for lexical resource integration on the Semantic Web, as part of the Linguistic Linked Open Data (LLOD) initiative, which aims to develop a Linked Open Data Subcloud of Linguistics (http://linguistics.okfn.org/resources/llod/). This resource thereby provides greater interoperability between existing lexical resources and the Semantic Web, and perhaps most importantly, addresses a gap in the LLOD cloud: although there are currently many lexical resources included in the LLOD cloud, previous efforts have not included information on syntactic behaviors and semantic roles, which are crucial for lexicalizing relational knowledge. While *lemonUby* has already taken advantage of the portions of past versions of SemLink included in UBY, continued efforts to integrate the current version of SemLink will allow for other valuable lexical information from both PropBank and the ON sense groupings to become part of the LLOD cloud.

## 5 Future Work: Expansion of SemLink

The primary goal for future work on SemLink is to expand the resource's coverage using the following methods. Firstly, additional annotations of the existing resources can be used to provide more comprehensive mappings. Secondly, the resources themselves can be improved to have greater coverage by adding to the types of annotation included in each. Finally, the addition of PB function tags (essentially semantic role labels) to numbered arguments allows for additional mappings. Each of these improvements is discussed in more detail in the sections to follow.

### 5.1 Expanding Coverage with Additional Annotations

We can firstly expand SemLink's coverage by focusing on cases where the corpus would have an annotation for one or more resources, but the mappings amongst all resources are incomplete. One of the most common cases of this type is where there is more than one FN frame associated with a particular VN class, requiring manual annotation of the most appropriate frame for a particular usage in the SemLink corpus. Approximately 50,000 of these cases have recently undergone annotation and simply require adjudication before being added to the next SemLink release. Similarly, other current annotation efforts include supplementing ON sense annotations where there are many senses associated with a given VN class.

We can also expand coverage by simply adding to the number of predicates included in an individual resource. We have started this process by examining which are the most frequent verbs in the SemLink corpus that are not included in VN. From this examination, we have discovered 20 verbs with PB annotations that are good candidates for addition to VN because they are relatively frequent in the corpus and would therefore greatly increase the full coverage of the resource: these instances make up 14,878, or 78%, of the 19,070 SemLink instances missing VN classes. These verbs include, for example, *account, be, benefit, cite, do, finance, let, market, tend, trigger,* and *violate*. Unfortunately, many of these verbs are not included in VN currently because their addition proved to be very difficult in the existing class structure: many do not readily fit into a VN class due to unique syntactic behaviors or semantic features, such as differing semantic roles. Nonetheless, 12 of these 20 verbs have already been situated in VN. Sometimes this required augmenting the existing class and subclass structure. For example, *discuss* is now found in the Chit_Chat class of VN, after some changes to the structure. In this case, the addition forced a reconsideration of the class structure, and in turn, a more rational organization for the class overall, with verbs in each of the two sibling classes fully functional in all the frames listed. The Seem class was also reorganized to more precisely capture the behavior of verbs in that class, and accommodate the extremely common verb, *be*, previously not included in VN. In other cases, entirely new classes have been added to accommodate some of these verbs. For example, the Benefit and Become classes have recently been added to VN, in order to house members such as *benefit, profit* and common copular senses of verbs like *become* and *get*.

### 5.2 Expanding Coverage with New Predicate Types

The second method for expanding the coverage of SemLink is to increase the number of predicate types included, which is extremely important for NLP applications. Firstly, the same event can be expressed with different parts of speech within a language; for example, *He feared the bear; His fear of bears; He is afraid of bears*. Secondly, the same event can be expressed with different parts of speech across languages, as demonstrated by the differences in the English, Hindi, and Arabic PBs. To move beyond syntactic idiosyncrasies to a deeper level of semantic representation, all of these predicate types should be included in NLP resources.

Currently, SemLink includes only verb predicates, because VN of course consists solely of verbs and PB consists largely of verbs. FN, in comparison, also includes nouns and adjectives. To address this gap, PB annotations have increasingly focused on noun and adjective predicate annotations. Guidelines for noun annotation have been developed over the past two years (guidelines available at http://verbs.colorado.edu/propbank/EPB-Annotation-Guidelines.pdf), and there are now approximately 48,000 noun annotations (although some of these simply note that the noun is not relational in the instance), and framesets for 2,549 nouns. The framesets borrow heavily from many of the frameset choices made by NomBank (Meyers et al., 2004), although the guidelines have some significant differences. Guidelines for adjective annotation are also being developed based on pilot annotations of about 5400 adjective predicates. Framesets for these adjectives are also currently being created, with 111 existing framesets. These new rolesets include mappings to FN frames and etymologically related VN classes, which will allow for future versions of SemLink to be efficiently updated.

Although separate framesets are created for each part of speech, each roleset also contains mappings to related rolesets of other parts of speech. Thus, for example, the adjective roleset absent.01 is linked to the noun roleset absence.01 and the verb roleset absent.01. Where possible, every effort is also made to ensure that the roleset itself is the same across these different parts of speech. These links allow for the creation of a unified set of framesets that represent all etymologically related realizations of the same concept across all parts of speech. This unification of PB rolesets is underway, so future versions of SemLink will be mapped to rolesets that are not tied to a particular part of speech, but rather represent a particular concept. This also facilitates the integration of PB and the Abstract Meaning Representation annotation project, the goal of which is to create a large-scale semantics bank (Banarescu et al., 2013).

### 5.3 Improving SemLink with PB Function Tags

Because of the differences in granularity represented by each lexical resource, there are often differences in the number of roles represented with a given predicate. PB lists roles that are found frequently with a given predicate and FN lists both 'Core' and 'Non-Core' roles separately. VN generally limits roles to those that are more 'core,' although of course this status is always debatable. As a result, there are often more roles listed in both PB and FN than in VN, and SemLink may miss links that can be made between PB and FN roles because of the gap in VN coverage. With numbered arguments alone, it can be difficult to make generalizations about PB arguments when they do not have a mapping to a VN theta role.

To address this difficulty and facilitate further mapping between FN and PB, the PB rolesets have been augmented with 'function tags' for all numbered arguments. These tags include all of PB's ArgM labels, as well as three additional tags: Proto-Agent, Proto-Patient, and Verb-Specific. These three tags are used, respectively, for Arg0, Arg1 and other arguments that simply don't have an appropriate function tag because they are quite unique to the verb in question. Each of the numbered arguments is currently being annotated with one of these function tags, allowing for users to replace the numbered args with these tags if so desired, even where a mapping to VN doesn't exist. For example, the roleset for *buy* would include the following function tags, indicated here by 'F':

**Buy.01**
Arg0: *Buyer*, F=Proto-Agent
Arg1: *Thing bought*, F=Proto-Patient
Arg2: *Seller*, F=Direction (used for source args)
Arg3: *Price paid*, F=Verb Specific
Arg4: *Benefactive*, F=Goal

Many of these function tags were added deterministically by using SemLink's mapping between PB arguments and VN roles. Each of the VN roles was mapped to a particular function tag; therefore, wherever there was an existing VN role mapping, this was used to supply the appropriate function tag. Manual annotations are complete for cases where there is no VN mapping.

These function tags will help to improve PB as a stand-alone corpus by allowing for the various higher-numbered arguments to be converted into more generalizable function tags. When using PB as training data, performance on Args 0 and 1 tends to be quite good because these arguments are syntactically and semantically very coherent; however, as mentioned previously, there is no consistent relationship between Args 2-5 and specific semantic roles. The function tags will facilitate useful groupings of these higher-numbered arguments. Within SemLink, the function tags can provide another level of potentially informative comparison between the more coarse-grained PB annotations and the more fine-grained roles of VN and FN, as well as overcoming gaps where a mapping to VN doesn't exist.

## 6 Conclusion

SemLink is a valuable tool that unifies several of the most important and comprehensive lexical resources, thereby combining the benefits of each. This unification and the mappings between resources allow for users to select the level of granularity most appropriate to their application, and to take advantage of annotations across resources. Improvements and expansions of each of the individual lexical resources included in SemLink will assist in increasing the coverage of SemLink itself, and continual updates to SemLink will ensure its quality despite ongoing changes in each of the individual lexicons and annotations included. Such improvements and expansions will allow for users to leverage the unique contributions of each of these complementary resources as each is expanded and refined. SemLink is a reminder and a reflection of the merit found in using resources in a complementary fashion: the whole, after all, can be greater than the sum of its parts. This lesson lies at the heart of linked data in linguistics, and SemLink provides a structure for greater integration of lexical resources into the Semantic Web.

## Acknowledgments

We gratefully acknowledge the support of the National Science Foundation Grant NSF-IIS-1116782, A Bayesian Approach to Dynamic Lexical Resources for Flexible Language Processing, and the support of DARPA FA8750-09-C-0179 (via BBN) Machine Reading: Ontology Induction and AMR and DARPA HR0011-11-C-0145 (via LDC) BOLT, as well as the generous assistance of Silvana Hartmann of Technische Universitat Darmstadt, an UBY collaborator. Any opinions, findings, and conclusions or recommendations expressed in this material are those of the authors and do not necessarily reflect the views of the National Science Foundation.

## References

L. Banarescu, C. Bonial, S. Cai, M. Georgescu, K. Griffitt, U. Hermjakob, K. Knight, P. Koehn, M. Palmer, and N. Schneider 2013. Abstract Meaning Representation for Sembanking. *Proceedings of the Linguistic Annotation Workshop.*

Dmitriy Dligach and Martha Palmer. 2011. Good Seed Makes a Good Crop: Accelerating Active Learning Using Language Modeling. *Proceedings of the 46th Annual Meeting of the Association for Computational Linguistics: Human Language Technologies.* Portland, OR.

David Dowty. 1991. Thematic Proto-roles and Argument Selection. *Language*, 67:547–619.

C.J. Duffield, J.D. Hwang, S.W. Brown, S.E. Viewig, J. Davis and M. Palmer. 2007. Criteria for the manual grouping of verb senses. *Proceedings of the Linguistic Annotation Workshop* Prague.

Judith Eckle-Kohler, Iryna Gurevychy, Silvana Hartmann, Michael Matuschek and Christian M. Meyer 2012. UBY-LMF A Uniform Model for Standardizing Heterogeneous Lexical-Semantic Resources in ISO-LMF. *Proceedings of the 8th International Conference on Language Resources and Evaluation (LREC)* Istanbul, Turkey.

Judith Eckle-Kohler, John Philip McCrae and Chrstian Chiarcos. submitted. *lemonUby* - a large, interlinked, syntactically-rich lexical resource for ontologies. submitted to *Semantic Web Journal*

Christiane Fellbaum (Ed.) 1998. *Wordnet: An Electronic Lexical Database.* MIT press, Cambridge.

Charles J Fillmore, Christoper R Johnson, and Miriam R L Petruck. 2002. Background to FrameNet. *International Journal of Lexicography*, 16(3):235–250.

Iryna Gurevychy, Judith Eckle-Kohler, Silvana Hartmann, Michael Matuschek, Christian M. Meyer, and Christian Wirth. 2012. UBY A Large-Scale Unified Lexical-Semantic Resource Based on LMF. *Proceedings of the 13th Conference of the European Chapter of the Association for Computational Linguistics (EACL)* Avignon, France t.

E. Joanis, Suzanne Stevenson, and D. James. 2008. A general feature space for automatic verb classification. *Natural Language Engineering.* 14(3):337-367.

Karin Kipper, Anna Korhonen, Neville Ryant and Martha Palmer. 2008. A large-scale classification of English verbs. *Language Resources and Evaluation Journal*, 42:21–40.

Anna Korhonen and T. Briscoe. 2004. Extended lexical-semantic classification of english verbs. *Proceedings of HLT/NAACL Workshop on Computational Lexical Semanticsl* Boston, Massachusetts.

Beth Levin. 1983. *English Verb Classes and Alternations: A Preliminary Investigation.* University of Chicago Press, Chicago.

Edward Loper, S. Yi, and Martha Palmer. 2007. Combining lexical resources: Mapping between PropBank and VerbNet. *Proceedings of the Seventh International Workshop on Computational Semantics (IWCS-7)* Tilburg.

Marcus M. Santorini and M.A. Marcinkiewicz. 1993. Building a Large Annotated Corpus of English: The Penn Treebank *Computational Linguistics*, 19(2):257–285.

John Philip McCrae, G. Aguado-de Cea, P. Buitelaar, P. Cimiano, T. Declerck, A. Gomez-Perez, J. Gracia, L. Hollink, E. Montiel-Ponsoda, D. Spohr, T. Wunner. 2012. Interchanging lexical resources on the Semantic Web. *Language Resources and Evaluation*, 46:701–719.

Merlo, P., and Van Der Plas, L. 2009. Abstraction and Generalization in Semantic Role Labels: PropBank, VerbNet or both? Proceedings of the 47th Annual Meeting of the ACL and 4th IJCNLP of the AFrameNetLP, Suntec, pp. 288-296.

Adam Meyers, R. Reeves, C. Macleod, R. Szekeley, V. Zielinska, B. Young and R. Grisham. 2004. The NomBank Project: An Interim Report *Proceedings of the Frontiers in Annotation Workshop, held in conjunction with HLT/NAACL 2004* Boston, Mass.

Martha Palmer, Daniel Gildea, and Paul Kingsbury. 2005. The Proposition Bank: An annotated corpus of semantic roles. *Computational Linguistics* 31(1):71–106.

Martha Palmer. 2009. Semlink: Linking PropBank, VerbNet and FrameNet. *Proceedings of the Generative Lexicon Conference* Pisa, Italy.

S. Pradhan, E.H. Hovy, M. Marcus, M. Palmer, L. Ramshaw and R. Weischedel. 2007. OntoNotes: A unified relational semantic representation. *Proceedings of the First IEEE International Conference on Semantic Computing(ICSC-07)* Irvine, CA.

Yi, S., Loper, E., and Palmer, M. 2007. Can semantic roles generalize across genres? Proceedings of the HLT/NAACL-2007, Rochester, pp. 548-555.

# LIME: Towards a Metadata Module for OntoLex

**Manuel Fiorelli**
University of Tor Vergata
Via del Politecnico 1, 00133
Rome, Italy
fiorelli@info.uniroma2.it

**Maria Teresa Pazienza**
University of Tor Vergata
Via del Politecnico 1, 00133
Rome, Italy
pazienza@info.uniroma2.it

**Armando Stellato**
University of Tor Vergata
Via del Politecnico 1, 00133
Rome, Italy
stellato@info.uniroma2.it

## Abstract

The OntoLex W3C Community Group has been working for more than a year on realizing a proposal for a standard ontology lexicon model. As the core-specification of the model is almost complete, the group started development of additional modules for specific tasks and use cases. We think that in many usage scenarios (e.g. linguistic enrichment, localization and alignment of ontologies) the discovery and exploitation of linguistically grounded datasets may benefit from summarizing information about their linguistic expressivity. While the VoID vocabulary covers the need for general metadata about linked datasets, this more specific information demands a dedicated extension. In this paper, we fill this gap by introducing LIME (Linguistic Metadata), a new vocabulary aiming at completing the OntoLex standard with specifications for linguistic metadata.

## 1 Introduction

Linguistic grounding of formalized knowledge is a long-standing principle in ontological modelling, at least traceable back to the "clarity criterion" (Gruber, 1995). Recently, natural language characterization of ontologies has proved useful both in the semantic reconciliation of heterogonous ontologies, and in many tasks interfacing natural language and ontologies, such as ontology verbalization, natural language ontology querying, ontology-based information extraction, ontology learning, validation and evolution.

Therefore, many research works aimed at defining common models and best-practices for linguistically grounding the Semantic Web, or even theorised a Linguistic Linked Open Data (Chiarcos, et al., 2012) cloud. The OntoLex W3C Community Group[1] is currently working on a principled ontology lexicon model that combines and improves previous proposals. Similarly, the Open Linguistics Working Group[2] of the Open Knowledge Foundation is pushing forward the publication of linguistic resources according to the Linked Open Data principles, thus developing a LOD (sub-)cloud of linguistic resources[3].

While focusing on representing linguistic information, existing proposals mostly overlook the characterization of ontologies, datasets and linguistic resources for what concerns their linguistic expressivity. This information should be provided in the form of metadata about linked data resources, providing summarizing information on how a dataset is linguistically represented, which formalism have been adopted, which languages have been used for representing its formal content and so on.

Such metadata would enable resolution strategies to be tuned to the specificities of a given task (e.g. is this a cross-language ontology alignment task?), and to retrieve suitable resources for supporting this resolution (e.g. is this a bi-lingual dictionary between the pair of languages used in a specific cross-language task?).

In this paper, we try to address the lack of a standardized vocabulary for linguistic metadata by proposing LIME, which is an abbreviation for **Li**nguistic **Me**tadata, which aims to become a module of the future OntoLex specification.

The rest of the paper is organized as follows. In section 2, we describe previous works on linguistic enrichment of ontologies/datasets and introduce the general usefulness of metadata in

[1] http://www.w3.org/community/ontolex/
[2] http://linguistics.okfn.org/
[3] http://nlp2rdf.lod2.eu/OWLG/llod/llod.svg

the Linked Data paradigm. In section 3, we introduce some application scenarios that would benefit from a dedicated vocabulary of linguistic metadata. In section 4, we describe the design of the vocabulary and some usages examples. Finally, in section 5, the conclusions.

## 2 Background and Related work

Currently, Knowledge Modelling languages for the Semantic Web do not support the representation of linguistic information to a large extent.

In RDF (Carroll & Klyne, 2004), natural language expressions are simply treated as language-tagged literals. RDFS (Guha & Brickley, 2004) provides standard properties for attaching these literals to conceptual resources as human-friendly names (`rdfs:label`) or longer narrative descriptions (`rdfs:comment`). SKOS (Bechhofer & Miles, 2009) introduces a finer-grain characterization of labels by means of a few sub-properties of `rdfs:label` accounting for differences at the terminological-correspondence level (Pastor-Sanchez, et al., 2009). SKOS-XL (W3C, 2009) models natural language expressions as individuals of a dedicated class (`skosxl:Label`). Providers of large KOSs (Hodge, 2000), such as AGROVOC (Caracciolo, et al., 2013) and EUROVOC (Paredes, et al., 2008), are widely adopting this modelling style, since they need to treat natural language expressions as "first-class citizens", at least for attaching editorial metadata to them. For instance, in the AGROVOC thesaurus, natural language labels are associated with a wide range of metadata, including creation/modification date and publication status, which are required for publication as well as for supporting the thesaurus collaborative development workflow (Caracciolo, et al., 2012).

Further works proposed even richer models for linguistically grounded ontologies/dataset. LingInfo (Buitelaar, et al., 2006) allows the description of the morphological and syntactic decomposition of natural language labels. On the other hand, LexOnto (Cimiano, et al., 2007) focuses on the mapping of linguistic predicate-argument structures to the join of semantic (binary) properties. Buitelaar et al. (2009) combined these two complementary models into a unified model, called LexInfo, highly based on the RDF porting of the LMF (Francopoulo, et al., 2006), thus benefitting from a principle conceptual model and higher compatibility with existing resources. These works informed the Lemon Model (Mccrae, et al., 2012) , which focuses on modularity and extensibility.

A complementary aspect consists in characterizing linguistic resources as a whole (Pazienza & Stellato, 2006b) with proper metadata.

A classification of linguistic resources (later backed by a suite of ontologies in (Pazienza, et al., 2008)), called Linguistic Watermark, was defined by us to support the development of a software library for accessing heterogeneous linguistic resources under a common API. A reflection mechanism in the library allows system and tools to access seamlessly different linguistic resources, understanding their nature, what these have to offer and exploiting their content in several application contexts.

The publication of linguistic resources (e.g. dictionaries, thesauri, corpora) as Linked Open Data is attracting the attention of Semantic Web practitioners. While using NLP tools to create semantic annotations with respect to formal ontologies, Kiryakov et al. (2004) advocated the representation in RDF of the linguistic resources that empower these tools, thus entailing a technological and a methodological reuse. When reconciling heterogeneous ontologies, linguistic resources may prove useful as well, since they provide a common grounding across different semantic theories, as they reflect the organic development of a language within a community.

The difficulties related to the triplification of linguistic resources is exemplified by the number of works that informed the development of the W3C RDF/OWL representation of WordNet (Van Assem, et al., 2006). WordNet, and similar resources, are not ontologies (Hirst, 2004), therefore any systematic translation into an ontology necessarily violates the formal semantics of the modelling language and ontological adequacy principles (Guarino & Welty, 2004). Gangemi et al. (2003a) restructured WordNet through the upper-ontology DOLCE (Gangemi, et al., 2002). OntoWordNet (Gangemi, et al., 2003b) is a notable output of this research line aiming at equipping WordNet with a formal semantics.

Another approach consists in a two-step process: produce an ontology modelling the core concepts found in the resource, then, instantiate that conceptual model with information found in a specific resource. The definition of a shared upper-model for linguistic resources is in fact another requirement of the forthcoming OntoLex model.

Concerning the importance of metadata in Linked Open Data, the necessity of summarizing information about a dataset as a whole has been considered and assessed. Jain et al. (2010) insisted on the lack of conceptual characterization of a dataset (e.g. what is it about?). Similar concerns motivated the development of VoID (Alexander, et al., 2011), a vocabulary for describing linked datasets.

In the field of Human Language Technology it has been promoted the reuse of Language Resources (LRs) through structured metadata. OLAC (Bird & Simons, 2003) extends the Dublin Core Metadata Element Set[4] for defining a simple template for the description of LRs that includes, among others, provenance metadata, resource typology and language identification. While OLAC aims at defining a distributed infrastructure for resource sharing, LRE Map (Calzolari, et al., 2012) is a crowd-sourced catalogue of LRs, initially fed by authors submitting papers to LREC Conferences. LRE Map defines numerous resource types and usage applications, whilst OLAC distinguishes a handful of types. Similar in scope to OLAC, META-SHARE (Piperidis, 2012) has its own metadata schema. In META-SHARE the taxonomy of LRs is not developed in a top-down manner, rather it originates from the adoption of metadata combination as a criterion for classifying LRs (Gavrilidou, et al., 2012).

These works have a wider scope than ours, as their definition of LRs include both software tools (e.g. postaggers and parsers) and data (e.g. corpus, dictionaries and grammars), managing heterogeneous formats. In contrast, we focus only on linguistic resources and linguistically enriched datasets, both expressed in RDF. Like META-SHARE we emphasize the importance of properties for the selection and interpretation of resources. Although Dublin Core can be used in conjunction with our model, we believe that some aspects, namely the provenance tracking, deserve dedicated models. Furthermore, our interest in quantitatively describing the extent to which a dataset has been lexicalized does not seem to be in the scope of these works.

It is worth of notice that these works are not grounded in the Semantic Web, as they do not use RDF for metadata representation nor their metadata are modelled using Semantic Web modelling languages. In fact, these works stress validation and mandatory nature of some metadata, something that is still being discussed within the Semantic Web community[5]. Despite being interesting, the broader definition of LR is out of the scope of most works about the representation of linguistic information as Linked Data, such as OntoLex.

## 3 Motivating Applications

Our previous research work with Linguistic Watermark revealed that many applications may benefit not only from a common linguistic model, but also from a shared (linguistic) metadata vocabulary for characterizing and summarizing the nature of linguistic resources.

In the following sections, we describe some use cases that would benefit from a metadata module, complementing the ontology lexicon model provided by the core OntoLex specification.

The requirement recurring in all scenarios is "discovery of (linguistic) resources", which is also the main requirement that motivated VoID. While providing a sound framework for coarse-grain description of datasets, VoID alone does not match this requirement, since it lacks vocabulary terms for language related metadata. These metadata should support both the description of linguistic resources, and the description of how ontologies and datasets have been enriched with their content.

### 3.1 Linguistic enrichment of ontologies

Algorithms and systems for automatically enriching ontologies with content from linguistic resources (Pazienza & Stellato, 2006a; Pazienza & Stellato, 2006c) may be written in terms of a common linguistic model, instead of being tightly coupled to specific resources.

In Figure 1, we see a screenshot of OntoLing (Pazienza & Stellato, 2005), a Protégé (Gennari, et al., 2003) plugin for the linguistic enrichment of ontologies. OntoLing uses metadata to uniformly load heterogeneous linguistic resources, by dynamically configuring its own UI to appropriately show their content and use it to enrich ontologies.

Discovery of linguistic resources can also be supported by linguistic metadata, provided in a way (e.g. in a VoID description) that can be recognized and indexed by Linked Data search engines. Agents may thus issue queries to these search engines to discover relevant linguistic resources in the LOD. The key point here is imme-

[4] http://dublincore.org/documents/dces

[5] https://www.w3.org/2012/12/rdf-val/

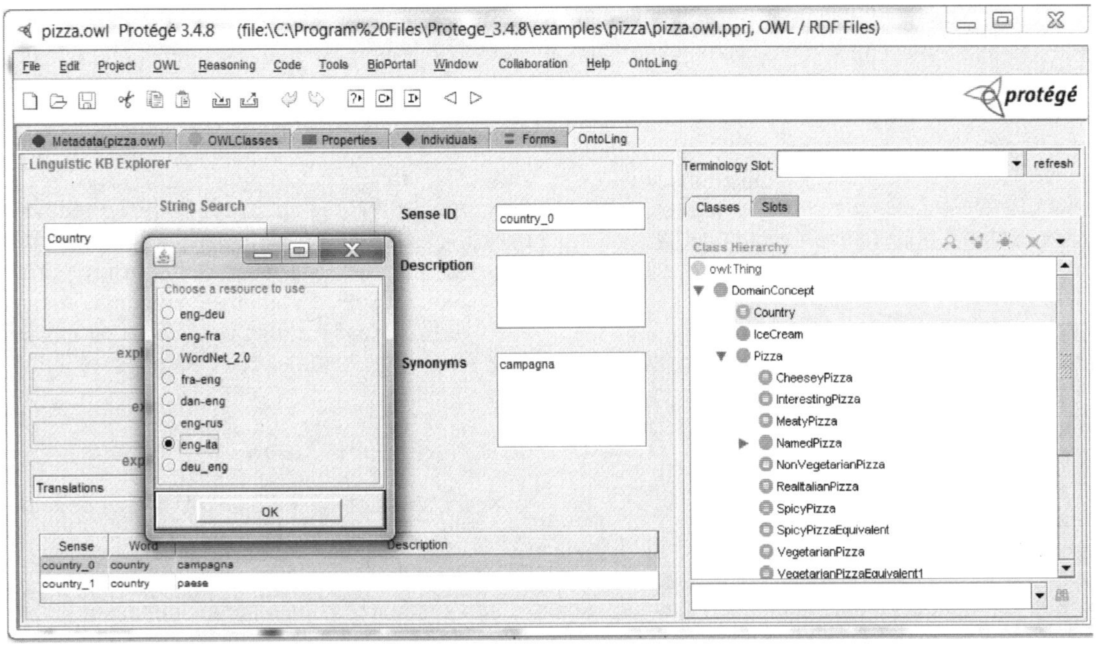


Figure 1. Loading different linguistic resources in OntoLing

diacy: in fact in a closed scenario an agent might profile the resources it controls by itself, while in open settings agents must necessarily depend on pre-compiled metadata to discover resources of interest.

### 3.2 Ontology Localization

Ontology Localization is about "the adaptation of an ontology to a particular language and culture" (Suárez-Figueroa & Gómez-Pérez, 2008). This definition was generalized by Cimiano et al. (2010), to account for variations in the cultural and socio-political context in a broader sense. They discussed thoroughly the interdependencies between the lexical and the conceptual layers, thus showing how an alteration of the former might require a modification of the latter, as well.

Nonetheless, bilingual dictionaries are valuable resources in an ontology localization process, as they provide translations of existing labels into the target natural language.

In this scenario, a localization agent might depend on linguistic metadata to determine its requirements, and, as discussed in previous section, query a LOD search engine for a list of matching resources. Semantically structured linguistic resources (such as the original WordNet for English, and the various wordnets created for many languages, such as EuroWordNet (Vossen, 1998) and Balkanet (Stamou, et al., 2002)) may help in understanding the conceptual heterogeneities which are bound to the different sociocultural contexts underlying each language.

### 3.3 Ontology Alignment

The Ontology Alignment task can benefit from a common metadata model.

Pazienza et al. (2007) extended the FIPA Ontology Service Specification with linguistically-aware methodologies for communication, describing a wide-scope framework for multi-agent systems design, semantic integration and coordination. In that perspective, Ontology Mediators should be able to understand which linguistic resources may be of support for a mediation activity between two ontologies/datasets. Such an understanding may happen at different levels, by making explicit the (natural) languages in which a given dataset is published, or the model being adopted for linguistically enriching the dataset. Even very specific facts, such as knowing that a certain popular resource (such as WordNet) has been used to support the lexicalization of a given dataset, may support the mediation activity: making the adoption of linguistic resources more explicit may be helpful in providing a common interlingua for aligning datasets sharing the same kind of linguistic development.

While Ontology Matching aims at supporting the automatic generation of alignments, a review of the state-of-the-art seems to support that in real scenarios the scarce availability of metadata hampers the achievement of this goal.

Shvaiko and Euzenat (2013) define the state-of-the-art in the field, by analysing the results of recent evaluation campaigns organized annually by the Ontology Alignment Evaluation Initiative[6] (OAEI). They stress the fact that no system outperforms the others in all matching scenarios, and that further advancement of the field requires the exploration of new paths. Among others, they cite the use of background knowledge and the design of meta-matchers able to construct the best strategy for solving a specific ontology alignment problem. We believe that for both purposes a metadata vocabulary may be useful, if not necessary, to describe a matching scenario, to plan a resolution strategy, and to support the discovery of relevant resources in the LOD cloud.

In the OAEI 2012 campaign (Shvaiko, et al., 2012), the Library track[7] provides evidences of the shortcomings in state-of-the-art matching systems. The track deals with two real-world thesauri encoded in SKOS: STW[8] (Neubert, 2009) for economics and TheSoz[9] (Zapilko, et al., 2013) for social sciences. Given the popularity of this genre of resources within large organizations and the growing adoption of SKOS, this track gives an important insight about the real-world performances of matching technologies. The results indicate clearly that current technologies (at least those participating in this international evaluation) have in fact some problems with these real-world matching scenarios. By first, most of the systems under evaluation were unable to deal with SKOS, therefore the organizers had to translate both thesauri into OWL. Unfortunately, this conversion can both introduce modelling errors, due to the stricter semantics of OWL, and cause loss of information, because the distinction between preferred and alternative labels is lost after the conversion. It turned out that the baseline matching all labels (both preferred and alternative ones) behaves more or less as the best system participating in the evaluation. This surprising result indicates that current matching strategies, developed for ontologies, are in fact quite inadequate for matching thesauri, which clearly deserve a special treatment. In this scenario, as evidenced by the contest results, terminology-based methods perform particularly well, and the importance of (linguistic) resources adopted in the alignment process seems to prevail over the adopted algorithms. Moreover, even for well-assessed multi-language resources, it should be noted that the quality of labels might vary drastically. For instance, both the thesauri used in the library track have been primarily developed in German, with translations made available in English. Therefore, it is unsurprising that German labels resulted sufficient alone for producing a good alignment, whereas English ones did not.

[6] http://oaei.ontologymatching.org/

[7] http://web.informatik.uni-mannheim.de/oaei-library/2012/

[8] http://zbw.eu/stw/versions/latest/about

[9] http://lod.gesis.org/thesoz/

## 4 Vocabulary Design

With the work on the core OntoLex specification going on, and after recognizing a clear need for a linguistic metadata vocabulary, we have revised our previous work on the Linguistic Watermark suite of vocabularies, aiming at the definition of a suitable metadata module for OntoLex. We called this module: LIME, which is an abbreviation for **Li**nguistic **Me**tadata[10]. As most metadata apply equally to ontologies representing conceptual knowledge, and datasets representing ground facts, in the forthcoming discussion we will use the term dataset to broadly refer to both.

In line with previous works on the general description of datasets, LIME has been defined as an extension of VoID. Accordingly, LIME metadata should be put in a VoID description of linguistically grounded resources.

By following the same approach adopted in Linguistic Watermark, we start by distinguishing metadata related to linguistic resources from metadata describing the linguistic expressivity of a dataset.

### 4.1 Linguistic Resources Metadata

There are a number of very simple facts that are relevant for assessing the usefulness of a linguistic resource in a task, which are practically missing from currently available metadata standards.

By first, the main discriminator for judging the usefulness of a linguistic resource in a given scenario is the set of (natural) *language(s)* it covers. Each of these languages should appear as a distinct value of the property `lime:language`. These values must conform to the specification of language tags in RDF. As natural language

[10] This name resembles Lemon, one of the various lexicon models which have informed the development of the OntoLex specification

```
Class: lime:LinguisticResource
  SubClassOf: void:Dataset
Class: lime:Dictionary
  SubClassOf: lime:LinguisticResource
Class: lime:SenseAwareDictionary
  SubClassOf: lime:Dictionary
Class: lime:ConceputalizedResource
  SubClassOf: lime:SenseAwareDictionary
Class: lime:MonolingualDictionary
  EquivalentClass: lime:Dictionary and lime:language exactly 1
Class: lime:BilingualDictionary
  EquivalentClass: lime:Dictionary and lime:language exactly 2
Class: lime:UnidirectionalBilingualDictionary
  SubClassOf:    lime:BilingualDictionary
  SubClassOf:    lime:sourceLanguage exactly 1
  SubClassOf:    lime:targetLanguage exactly 1
  DisjointWith: lime:BidirectionalBilingualDictionary
Class: lime:BidirectionalBilingualDictionary
  SubClassOf:    lime:BilingualDictionary
  DisjointWith: limeUnidirectionalBilingualDictionary
Class: lime:ConsistentBidirectionalBilingualDictionary
  SubClassOf:    lime:BidirectionalBilingualDictionary
DataProperty: lime:language
  Range: xsd:string
DataProperty: lime:sourceLanguage
  SubPropertyOf: lime:language
DataProperty: lime:targetLanguage
  SubPropertyOf: lime:language
```

Figure 2. An excerpt of the LIME vocabulary definition expressed in Manchester Syntax

expressions are usually hold by language tagged literals, this design avoids the need for a suitable mapping for relating metadata to data. This property does not hold when relying on other identification mechanisms, including the use of URIs[11].

Currently, no standard RDF vocabulary provides summarizing information about the coverage of natural language expressions in a dataset. In particular, Linguistic Resources should also be classifiable (see Figure 2) as *monolingual*, *bilingual* (as of translation resources), or *multilingual*.

Bilingual dictionaries are a kind of lexical resource providing direct translations between terms. These resources are modelled as individuals of `lime:BilingualDictionary`, which extends the class `lime:Dictionary`. These translations may or may not be divided according to the senses of the input terms (e.g. consider a popular free bilingual dictionary such Freelang[12] for the first case, and most of the FreeDict[13] dictionaries for the latter). To account for this difference, we have introduced the class `lime:SenseAwareDictionary`.

The translations may be available in one direction only (`lime:UnidirectionalBilingualDictionary`), or allow to go from each of the two languages to the other one (`lime:BidirectionalBilingualDictionary`). These two classes are declared disjoint. Concerning directional resources, we have defined two properties `lime:sourceLanguage` and `lime:targetLanguage`, which reflect the direction of the translation. Symmetry may be guaranteed or not (e.g. some dictionaries may not guarantee that an inverse translation of a translated term always brings back to the original term).

Resources with a strong conceptual backbone (`lime:ConceptualizedResource`) may provide consistent multilingual denotation of their entries. In this sense, any multilingual SKOS concept scheme with a strong linguistic grounding could be classified as a multilingual linguistic

[11] Look at http://www.lexvo.org/ for an example

[12] http://www.freelang.net/

[13] http://freedict.org

resource. The metadata model should be as agnostic with respect to the resource theory as possible, while still being able to tell whether a conceptualization of any kind exists. The metadata should describe to which extent the conceptualization is structured. For instance, the property `lime:hasTaxonomy` tells whether lexical concepts are organized into a taxonomy or not. In our model conceptualized resources are subclass of sense-aware dictionaries, as each attachment of a natural language expression to a concept corresponds to a distinguished sense of that expression. Other properties should trivially tell whether certain information is available or not, so that systems may know what to rely on. An example could be knowing that a given dictionary provides glosses (`lime:hasGlosses`) or usage examples (`lime:hasUsageExamples`). Furthermore, we assume that glosses and examples are attached either to senses in sense-aware resources, or to words otherwise.

### 4.2 OntoLinguistic Metadata

Whether a given dataset adopts vocabularies for an elaborated linguistic description (such as SKOS-XL or the under-development OntoLex) or just relies on simple labelling primitives, it is important to describe these facts through proper metadata. Thus, while the previous metadata relate to the description of linguistic resources (expressed as linked data), the onto-linguistic metadata provide quantitative and qualitative information about the linguistic expressivity of any linked dataset.

As for linguistic resources, the very first fact that should be declared about a dataset consists in the languages (`lime:language`) in which it is expressed. In the context of an alignment process, this enables immediate verification of the linguistic-compatibility between datasets. Obviously, the sole fact that lexicalizations exist for a given language is not enough for telling whether that language is sufficiently covering and representing the conceptual content of the resource.

In particular, for each language, the metadata should provide the percentage of RDF resources, per type (classes, individuals, properties, SKOS concepts) described by at least a lexicalization in that language. Additional information, such as the average number of lexicalizations per resource, may provide more insights on the "weight" of a language in describing the resource.

The following RDF snippet illustrates the use of LIME for asserting that English lexicalizations cover 75% (`lime:percentage`) of the SKOS concepts in the dataset `:dat`, and that there are, on average, 3.5 English lexical entries per concept.

```
:dat lime:languageCoverage [
  lime:lang "en";
  lime:resourceCoverage [
    lime:class skos:Concept;
    lime:percentage 0.75;
    lime:avgNumOfEntries 3.5
  ]
].
```

We use OWL 2 to restrict the range of `lime:percentage` to the interval [0.0, 1.0].

```
lime:percentage a
    owl:DatatypeProperty;
  rdfs:range [
    rdf:type rdfs:Datatype ;
    owl:onDatatype xsd:float ;
    owl:withRestrictions (
      [xsd:minInclusive 0.0]
      [xsd:maxInclusive 1.0]
    )
  ].
```

The range of `lime:avgNumOfEntries` is similarly restricted to non-negative floats.

```
lime:avgNumOfEntries a
    owl:DatatypeProperty;
  rdfs:range [
    rdf:type rdfs:Datatype ;
    owl:onDatatype xsd:float ;
    owl:withRestrictions (
      [xsd:minInclusive 0.0]
    )
  ].
```

The inclusion of zero in both ranges allows the representation of the lack of lexicalizations in a given natural language.

The grounding of two datasets to a common natural language allows them to be compared on the basis of the implicit knowledge about the use of that language by the community of its speakers. However, if mappings to popular (conceptualized) linguistic resources are represented explicitly, then these resources may be exploited as a kind of semantic hub between any two datasets sharing the same linguistic development. Being these resources a sort of less-ambiguous interlingua, the metadata about their usage are in fact very similar to the ones we have mentioned for natural languages. Below we reframe the previous example by considering the enrichment of a dataset with links to synsets from WordNet.

```
:dat
 lime:lexicalResourceCoverage [
```

```
    lime:lexresource
       ewn:WordNet;
    lime:resourceCoverage [
      lime:class skos:Concept;
      lime:lexConceptClass
                       wn:Synset;
      lime:percentage 0.75;
      lime:avgNumOfEntries 3.5
    ]
  ].
```

The property `lime:lexConceptClass` informs the LIME consumer of the specific class of the linguistic resource which is subclassing the generic OntoLex class `ontolex:LexicalConcept`.

The presence of any linguistic description does not guarantee that an agent might exploit it. Indeed, the agent must know whether linguistic information is available in the form of traditional `rdfs:label`s, SKOS labels, SKOS-XL reified labels, or OntoLex attachments. Most datasets are likely to use multiple linguistic models simultaneously, each one for different needs (e.g. the distinction between preferred and alternative labels may be or not of interest). These models are hold by the property `lime:linguisticModel`, which extends the property `void:vocabulary`, as the former expresses a more specific association with the vocabulary. When a dataset adopts multiple linguistic models, we assume that they express the same information about the metadata terms that apply to them. For instance, when both SKOS and RDFS are used (the latter being possibly materialized from the former), they must express the same labels, though RDFS loses the SKOS-specific finer grain distinctions.

Finally, the metadata vocabulary should account for the widely adopted practice of using evocative names as local name of the resources URIs. Local names are often not natural language expressions per se, since they are constrained by limitations of the URI syntax or by some naming convention. Luckily, the relation between local names and natural language expressions is generally very simple. Moreover, it is often expressed through a limited set of common patterns (e.g. camel-case, underscore separated words). These simple relations might be modelled through simple transducers, perhaps finite state ones. LIME provides default transducers for some of this popular naming schemes.

Local names are the weakest mechanism for linguistic enrichment, as synonymy and multilingualism are hardly supported. Actually, local names mostly serve as an aid for knowledge developers, who can get a sense of the data they are working on, without the need of considering complex lexicalization models. Therefore, some metadata should express whether (cleaned) local names are subsumed or not by lexicalizations provided in other manners.

## 5 Conclusion

In this paper, we presented LIME, a vocabulary for **Li**nguistic **Me**tadata, which aims to become a standard module of the OntoLex model.

Relevant metadata include statistics about natural language lexicalisations and mappings to linguistic resources. By following the same approach used in VoID, we defined dedicated terms, instead of relying on a fully-fledged (but maybe harder to parse) statistical vocabulary. However, as Data Cube (Cyganiak & Reynolds, 2013) establishes for the representation of (statistical) multi-dimensional data, we should consider providing mappings to it, or even adopting it.

While at present the coverage of a linguistic resource is interpreted only with respect to explicit mappings to its conceptual content, we could consider as well to define a merely lexical coverage. This information correlates with the linguistic compatibility of two datasets, as well can guide their linguistic enrichment to increase such compatibility, when it appears to be low.

An extension of LIME could attempt to go beyond simple coverage statistics, and try to capture the quality of linguistic information in deeper ways. By first, we should agree on a definition of quality, perhaps as some confidence measure. Then, we should decide the granularity of the metadata, i.e. whether to quantify the overall confidence of the linguistic description, or to qualify each linguistic attachment individually.

While developing LIME, we discussed about the very nature of linguistic resources, and how they relate to terminological thesauri or even just lexicalized conceptualizations. Actually, answering these questions is fundamental for the advancement of the field of ontology lexicalization.

## Acknowledgements

This research has been partially supported by the EU project SemaGrow (Grant agreement no: 318497).

## References

Alexander, K., Cyganiak, R., Hausenblas, M., & Zhao, J. (2011, March 3). *Describing Linked Datasets with the VoID Vocabulary (W3C Interest*

*Group Note).* Retrieved May 16, 2012, from World Wide Web Consortium (W3C): http://www.w3.org/TR/void/

Bechhofer, S., & Miles, A. (2009, aug). *SKOS Simple Knowledge Organization System Reference.* W3C Recommendation, W3C.

Bird, S., & Simons, G. (2003). Extending Dublin Core Metadata to Support the Description and Discovery of Language Resources. *Computers and the Humanities, 37*(4), 375-388.

Buitelaar, P., Cimiano, P., Haase, P., & Sintek, M. (2009). Towards Linguistically Grounded Ontologies. *In Proceedings of the 6th Annual European Semantic Web Conference (ESWC2009),* (pp. 111-125).

Buitelaar, P., Declerck, T., Frank, A., Racioppa, S., Kiesel, M., Sintek, M., . . . Cimiano, P. (2006). LingInfo: Design and Applications of a Model for the Integration of Linguistic Information in Ontologies. *OntoLex06.* Genoa, Italy.

Calzolari, N., Del Gratta, R., Francopoulo, G., Mariani, J., Rubino, F., Russo, I., & Soria, C. (2012). The LRE Map. Harmonising Community Descriptions of Resources. *Proceedings of the Eighth International Conference on Language Resources and Evaluation (LREC-2012)* (pp. 1084-1089). ELRA.

Caracciolo, C., Stellato, A., Morshed, A., Johannsen, G., Rajbhandari, S., Jaques, Y., & Keizer, J. (2013). The AGROVOC Linked Dataset. (P. Hitzler, & K. Janowicz, Eds.) *Semantic Web Journal, 4*(3), 341–348. doi:10.3233/SW-130106

Caracciolo, C., Stellato, A., Rajbahndari, S., Morshed, A., Johannsen, G., Keizer, J., & Jacques, Y. (2012, August Tuesday, 14). Thesaurus Maintenance, Alignment and Publication as Linked Data. *International Journal of Metadata, Semantics and Ontologies (IJMSO), 7*(1), 65-75.

Carroll, J. J., & Klyne, G. (2004, feb). *Resource Description Framework (RDF): Concepts and Abstract Syntax.* W3C Recommendation, W3C.

Chiarcos, C., Nordhoff, S., & Hellmann, S. (Eds.). (2012). *Linked Data in Linguistics.* Springer.

Cimiano, P., Haase, P., Herold, M., Mantel, M., & Buitelaar, P. (2007). LexOnto: A Model for Ontology Lexicons for Ontology-based NLP. *In Proceedings of the OntoLex07 Workshop (held in conjunction with ISWC'07).*

Cimiano, P., Montiel-Ponsoda, E., Buitelaar, P., Espinoza, M., & Gómez-Pérez, A. (2010, April). A note on ontology localization. *Applied Ontology, 5*(2), 127-137.

Cyganiak, R., & Reynolds, D. (2013). *The RDF Data Cube Vocabulary.* W3C.

Francopoulo, G., George, M., Calzolari, N., Monachini, M., Bel, N., Pet, M., & Soria, C. (2006). Lexical Markup Framework (LMF). *LREC2006.* Genoa, Italy.

Gangemi, A., Guarino, N., Masolo, C., & Oltramari, A. (2003). Sweetening WORDNET with DOLCE. *AI Magazine, 24*(3), 13-24.

Gangemi, A., Guarino, N., Masolo, C., Oltramari, A., & Schneider, L. (2002). Sweetening ontologies with DOLCE. In *Knowledge engineering and knowledge management: Ontologies and the semantic Web* (pp. 166-181). Springer.

Gangemi, A., Navigli, R., & Velardi, P. (2003). The OntoWordNet Project: extension and axiomatization of conceptual relations in WordNet. In *On the move to meaningful internet systems 2003: CoopIS, DOA, and ODBASE* (pp. 820-838). Springer.

Gavrilidou, M., Labropoulou, P., Desipri, E., Piperidis, S., Papageorgiou, H., Monachini, M., . . . Mapelli, V. (2012). The META-SHARE Metadata Schema for the Description of Language Resources. *Proceedings of the Eighth International Conference on Language* (pp. 1090-1097). ELRA.

Gennari, J., Musen, M., Fergerson, R., Grosso, W., Crubézy, M., Eriksson, H., . . . Tu, S. (2003). The evolution of Protégé-2000: An environment for knowledge-based systems development,. *International Journal of Human-Computer Studies, 58*(1), 89–123.

Gruber, T. R. (1995). Toward principles for the design of ontologies used for knowledge sharing. *International Journal of Human-Computer Studies, 43*(5-6), 907-928.

Guarino, N., & Welty, C. (2004). An Overview of OntoClean. In S. Staab, & R. Studer (Eds.), *The Handbook on Ontologies* (pp. 151-172). Berlin: Springer-Verlag.

Guha, R. V., & Brickley, D. (2004, feb). *RDF Vocabulary Description Language 1.0: RDF Schema.* W3C Recommendation, W3C.

Hirst, G. (2004). Ontology and the Lexicon. In S. Staab, & R. Studer (Eds.), *Handbook on Ontologies* (pp. 209-230). Springer.

Hodge, G. (2000, April). *Systems of Knowledge Organization for Digital Libraries: Beyond Traditional Authority Files.* Washington, DC: Council on Library and Information Resources.

Jain, P., Hitzler, P., Yeh, P. Z., Verma, K., & Sheth, A. P. (2010). Linked Data Is Merely More Data. *AAAI Spring Symposium: Linked Data Meets Artificial Intelligence.* AAAI Press.

Kiryakov, A., Popov, B., Terziev, I., Manov, D., & Ognyanoff, D. (2004). Semantic annotation, indexing, and retrieval. *Web Semantics: Science, Services and Agents on the World Wide Web, 2*(1), 49-79.

Mccrae, J., Aguado-De-Cea, G., Buitelaar, P., Cimiano, P., Declerck, T., Gómez-Pérez, A., . . . Wunner, T. (2012, dec). Interchanging lexical resources on the Semantic Web. *Lang. Resour. Eval., 46*(4), 701-719.

Neubert, J. (2009). Bringing the "Thesaurus for Economics" on to the Web of Linked Data. In C. Bizer, T. Heath, T. Berners-Lee, & K. Idehen (Ed.), *Proceedings of the Linked Data on the Web Workshop (LDOW2009). 538.* Madrid, Spain: CEUR-WS.org.

Paredes, L. P., Rodrıguez, J. M., & Azcona, E. R. (2008). Promoting Government Controlled Vocabularies for the Semantic Web: the EUROVOC Thesaurus and the CPV Product Classification System. *Semantic Interoperability in the European Digital Library*, (p. 111).

Pastor-Sanchez, J.-A., Martínez Mendez, F. J., & Rodríguez-Muñoz, J. V. (2009). Advantages of thesaurus representation using the Simple Knowledge Organization System (SKOS) compared with proposed alternatives. *Information Research, 14*(4), 10.

Pazienza, M. T., & Stellato, A. (2005). The Protégé Ontoling Plugin - Linguistic Enrichment of Ontologies in the Semantic Web. *In poster proceedings of the 4th International Semantic Web Conference (ISWC-2005).* Galway, Ireland.

Pazienza, M. T., Stellato, A., & Turbati, A. (2008). Linguistic Watermark 3.0: an RDF framework and a software library for bridging language and ontologies in the Semantic Web. *Semantic Web Applications and Perspectives, 5th Italian Semantic Web Workshop (SWAP2008).* FAO-UN, Rome, Italy.

Pazienza, M., & Stellato, A. (2006). An Environment for Semi-automatic Annotation of Ontological Knowledge with Linguistic Content. In Y. Sure, & J. Domingue (A cura di), *The Semantic Web: Research and Applications, 3rd European Semantic Web Conference, ESWC 2006, Budva, Montenegro, June 11-14, 2006, Proceedings. Lecture Notes in Computer Science. 4011*, p. 442-456. Springer.

Pazienza, M., & Stellato, A. (2006). Exploiting Linguistic Resources for building linguistically motivated ontologies in the Semantic Web. *Second Workshop on Interfacing Ontologies and Lexical Resources for Semantic Web Technologies (OntoLex2006).* Genoa, Italy.

Pazienza, M., & Stellato, A. (2006). Linguistic Enrichment of Ontologies: a methodological framework. *Second Workshop on Interfacing Ontologies and Lexical Resources for Semantic Web Technologies (OntoLex2006).* Genoa, Italy.

Pazienza, M., Sguera, S., & Stellato, A. (2007, December 26). Let's talk about our "being": A linguistic-based ontology framework for coordinating agents. (R. Ferrario, & L. Prévot, Eds.) *Applied Ontology, special issue on Formal Ontologies for Communicating Agents, 2*(3-4), 305-332.

Piperidis, S. (2012). The META-SHARE Language Resources Sharing Infrastructure: Principles, Challenges, Solutions. *Proceedings of the Eighth International Conference on Language* (pp. 36-42). ELRA.

Shvaiko, P., & Euzenat, J. (2013). Ontology Matching: State of the Art and Future Challenges. *IEEE Transactions on Knowledge and Data Engineering, 25*(1), 158-176.

Shvaiko, P., Euzenat, J., Kementsietsidis, A., Mao, M., Noy, N., & Stuckenschmidt, H. (Eds.). (2012). Proceedings of the 7th International Workshop on Ontology Matching, Boston, MA, USA, November 11, 2012. *OM. 946.* CEUR-WS.org.

Stamou, S., Oflazer, K., Pala, K., Christoudoulakis, D., Cristea, D., Tufiş, D., . . . Grigoriadou, M. (2002). BALKANET: A Multilingual Semantic Network for the Balkan Languages. *International Wordnet Conference*, (pp. 12-14). Mysore, India.

Suárez-Figueroa, M. C., & Gómez-Pérez, A. (2008). First Attempt towards a Standard Glossary of Ontology Engineering Terminology. In B. N. Madsen, & H. E. Thomsen (Eds.), *Managing Ontologies and Lexical Resources. TKE 2008 8th International Conference on Terminology and KE.* Copenhagen: Institut for Internationale Sprogstudier og Vidensteknologi (ISV).

Van Assem, M., Gangemi, A., & Schreiber, G. (2006). Conversion of WordNet to a standard RDF/OWL representation. *Proceedings of the Fifth International Conference on Language Resources and Evaluation (LREC'06), Genoa, Italy.*

Vossen, P. (1998). *EuroWordNet: A Multilingual Database with Lexical Semantic Networks.* Dordrecht: Kluwer Academic Publishers.

W3C. (2009, August 18). *SKOS Simple Knowledge Organization System eXtension for Labels (SKOS-XL).* (A. Miles, & S. Bechhofer, Eds.) Retrieved March 22, 2011, from World Wide Web Consortium (W3C): http://www.w3.org/TR/skos-reference/skos-xl.html

Zapilko, B., Schaible, J., Mayr, P., & Mathiak, B. (2013). TheSoz: A SKOS Representation of the Thesaurus for the Social Sciences. (P. Hitzler, & K. Janowicz, Eds.) *Semantic Web Journal, 4*(3), 257–263.

# Lemon-aid: using Lemon to aid quantitative historical linguistic analysis

**Steven Moran**
University of Zurich
University of Marburg
steven.moran@uzh.ch

**Martin Brümmer**
University of Leipzig
AKSW
bruemmer@informatik.uni-leipzig.de

**Abstract**

In this short paper, we describe how we converted dictionary and wordlist data made available by the QuantHistLing project into the Lexicon Model for Ontologies. By doing so, we leverage Linked Data to combine disparate lexical resources – more than fifty lexicons and dictionaries – by converting the lexical data into an RDF model that is specified by Lemon. The resulting new Linked Data resource, what we call the QHL dataset, provides researchers with a *translation graph*, which allows users to query across the underlying lexicons and dictionaries to extract semantically-aligned wordlists.

## 1 Introduction

There is an increasing amount of research that applies quantitative approaches to historical-comparative linguistic processes, including diverse areas such as: statistical tests for genealogical relatedness (Kessler, 2001), methods for phylogenetic reconstruction (Holman et al., 2011; Bouckaert et al., 2012), phonetic alignment algorithms (Kondrak, 2000; Prokić et al., 2009), and automatic detection of cognates (Turchin et al., 2010; Steiner et al., 2011), borrowings (Nelson-Sathi et al., 2011), and proto-forms (Bouchard-Côté et al., 2013). However, before any of these steps within the pipeline of computational historical linguistics can be undertaken, lexical data from secondary resources such as dictionaries and wordlists, or from tertiary resources like online lexical databases, must be collected, digitized and collated. The promise of the automatization of time-consuming tasks, such as lexical comparison, phonetic alignments and similarity judgements, is providing a resurgence of historical-comparative analysis, the goal of which is to identify the genealogical relatedness of languages and ultimately inform the prehistory of native peoples and their migrations. By linking data on these low-resource languages to the Linguistic Linked Open Data cloud (LLOD), and thus to the Linked Open Data cloud (LOD), we are also following in the practice and vision of the Semantic Web – open data sharing.

In the following sections we describe the QHL project's lexicon and wordlist format and how we converted the data into our ontological model specified in Lemon (McCrae et al., 2010; McCrae et al., 2011). The resulting resource allows users to query across what are originally disparate paper lexicons and dictionaries to extract semantically-aligned wordlists for historical-comparative analysis. We provide some examples in SPARQL.

## 2 Data

### 2.1 Source

The Quantitative Historical Linguistics (QuantHistLing) research unit aims to uncover and clarify phylogenetic relationships between native South American languages using quantitative methods.[1] There are two main objectives of the project: digitalization of lexical resources on South American languages and the development of computer-assisted methods and algorithms to quantitatively analyze the digitized data. The project aims to digitize around 500 works, most of which are currently only available in print and many of which are the only resources available for the languages that they describe. The list of the languages, language families and the data that has so far been digitized is available online.[2]

The QuantHistLing project has a simple data output format that contains metadata (prefixed with "@") and tab-delimited lexical out-

[1] http://quanthistling.info/

[2] http://quanthistling.info/index.php?id=resources

put. An example is given in Figure 1. The first row following the metadata contains the data header with the fields: QLCID, HEAD, HEAD_DOCULECT, TRANSLATION, TRANSLATION_DOCULECT, which correspond respectively to the internal QLC unique identifier, the headword in the dictionary, the *doculect* of the headword (or in other words the language in which this particular document describes), the translation for the given headword, and the doculect that the translation is given in. For each resource a data dump with the same format is provided by the project.

### 2.2 Conversion

We convert the QLC data into Linked Data that conforms to the Lemon model with a simple Python script. Lemon is an ontological model for modeling lexicons and machine-readable dictionaries for linking to the Semantic Web and the Linked Data cloud.[3] It is based on the Lexical Markup Framework (LMF) (Francopoulo et al., 2006) and uses the idea of data categories (Romary, 2010), like ISOCat (Kemps-Snijders et al., 2008), which include uniquely identified concepts that are useful for computational tasks (McCrae et al., 2011).

The benefits of modeling lexical data in Lemon are multi-fold. Internal to the Lemon mission are the benefits from overcoming the challenges that the model was designed to meet:[4]

- RDF-native form to enable leverage of existing Semantic Web technologies (SPARQL, OWL, RIF etc.).
- Linguistically sound structure based on LMF to enable conversion to existing offline formats.
- Separation of the lexicon and ontology layers, to ensure compatability with existing OWL models.
- Linking to data categories, in order to allow for arbitrarily complex linguistic description. In particular the LexInfo vocabulary is aligned to Lemon and ISOcat.
- A small model using the principle of least power - the less expressive the language, the more reusable the data.

We chose to model lexicons in Lemon instead of the Graph Annotation Format (GrAF) (Ide and Suderman, 2007) and the Lexicon Interchange FormaT (LIFT)[5] because of Lemon's tight integration with Semantic Web technologies, which allows us to add lexical data to the Linked Open Data cloud (LOD) and the Linguistic Linked Open Data cloud (LLOD). From the perspective of linguistics researchers, mapping dictionary and wordlists data to the LLOD has many advantages:

- Data that is linked is available on the Web in a standard format and accessible via the (L)LOD.
- Data are queryable through a SPARQL endpoint.
- The use of an ontology and Linked Data addresses the problem of merging disparate dictionary entries using senses and meaning mappings, including leveraging other sources such as Wordnet and domain-specific ontologies.

### 2.3 Ontology

Figure 2 illustrates our model implementation of the Lemon model with the QHL data.[6] Subjects, predicates and objects are clearly labeled. Currently the dataset contains 3,828,420 triples and we have made links to Lexvo,[7] a pivot for linguistic resources in the LLOD, via ISO 639-3 language name identifiers (de Melo, Submittied). There are currently 216 language links to Lexvo and thus numerous entries to other language resources.

## 3 Application

A major goal in historical-comparative linguistics is the identification of cognates, i.e. sets of words in genealogically related languages that have been derived from a common word or root (e.g. English 'is', German 'ist', Latin 'est', from Indo-European 'esti'). Modeling dictionaries and lexicons in a pivot ontology using overlaps in translations is

[3]The Lemon developers are also active in the W3C Ontology-Lexica Community Group, whose goal is to "develop models for the representation of lexica (and machine readable dictionaries) relative to ontologies". See: `http://www.w3.org/community/ontolex/`.

[4]`http://lemon-model.net/`

[5]`https://code.google.com/p/lift-standard/`

[6]Our version of the Linked Data is available here: `http://linked-data.org/datasets/qhl.ttl.zip`.

[7]`http://www.lexvo.org/`

Figure 1: QLC data format

```
@date: 2012-11-23
@url: http://www.quanthistling.info/data/source/aguiar1994/dictionary-329-369.html
@source_title: Analise descritiva e teorica do Katukino-Pano
@source_author: de Aguiar, Maria Sueli
@source_year: 1994
@doculect: Katukina, n/a, Katukina, Panoan
@doculect: Portugues, por, Portugues, Panoan
QLCID HEAD HEAD_DOCULECT TRANSLATION TRANSLATION_DOCULECT
aguiar1994/329/1 ai Katukina presente Portugues
aguiar1994/329/2 aima Katukina solteiro Portugues
aguiar1994/329/3 ain Katukina esposa Portugues
aguiar1994/329/4 ainnan Katukina cipo para cesta Portugues
aguiar1994/329/5 ainnan Katukina casado Portugues
aguiar1994/329/6 aka Katukina soco Portugues
aguiar1994/329/7 akaai Katukina tomar Portugues
```

Figure 2: Implementation of QHL data in Lemon

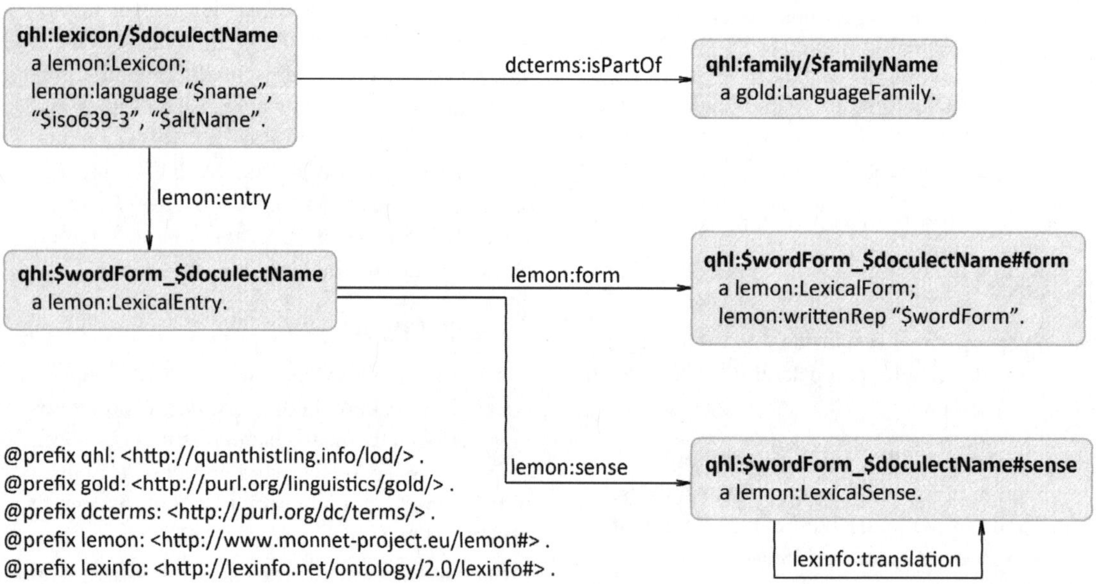

one way to merge several resources into one RDF graph for querying and extracting semantically-aligned wordlists, which can then be used as input into computational historical linguistics tools such as LingPy (List and Moran, 2013).[8]

As a first step, we have converted the QHL data into Linked Data and it is available online through a SPARQL endpoint.[9] Querying the combined dictionaries and lexicons is straightforward, as shown in example 1, which returns us all triples.

(1)
```
select * where
{GRAPH
<http://quanthistling.info/lod/>
{?s ?p ?o}
}
```

Next we limit the query in example 2 to the set of languages in our translation graph that contain written forms for the lexical sense "casa". The query returns pairs of words, but one can programmatically expand it by using the *wordForm2* and inserting it in the filter clause.

(2)
```
PREFIX lemon:
<http://www.monnet-project.eu/lemon#>
PREFIX lexinfo:
<http://lexinfo.net/ontology/2.0/
lexinfo#>
select ?wordForm1 ?language1
?wordForm2 ?language2 where
{GRAPH
<http://quanthistling.info/lod/>
{
?word1 a lemon:LexicalForm;
lemon:writtenRep ?wordForm1.
?entry1 lemon:form ?word1;
lemon:sense ?sense1.
?language1 lemon:entry ?entry1.
?sense1 lexinfo:translation ?sense2.
?word2 a lemon:LexicalForm;
lemon:writtenRep ?wordForm2.
?entry2 lemon:form ?word2;
lemon:sense ?sense2.
?language2 lemon:entry ?entry2.
FILTER(str(?wordForm1)="casa")
}
}
```

Regarding our use of *sense*, the Lemon documentation states: "The sense object represents a mapping between a lexical entry and an ontology entity." The "ontology entity" that the Lemon authors use as an example is a link to the corresponding DBpedia or Wiktionary entry, where a description of the meaning can be found. While the principle is sound, this information is not contained in our data. Hence that is why there is no more information in our #sense resources. If a reference to an ontology entry is to be added later, it can be easily done so by adding it as a property of the #sense resource (for example as owl:sameAs, dcterms:references, etc.). However, if we have only strings in languages that are very rare, how are we to add an ontology entry? For most of the entries, there will be no corresponding entry. In fact, suppose we find the translation of an entry in a poorly documented language into a richer-resourced language (e.g. Katukina to Portuguese), we would not know if the Portuguese sense is a proper description of the sense of the work in Katukina. Moreover, the links would be sparse and some, if not many, would be wrong due to missing information. Therefore, our modelling follows the Lemon cookbook (examples 29, page 18) for good reason: the translation of a word is neither a translation of its wordform or representation nor is it a translation of its lexical entry. It is thus linguistically sound to say the "sense" of a word like "casa" is translated into another language, but its word form or entry is not.

Building on the former query, one can also add a node, as illustrated in example 3:[10]

(3)
```
PREFIX lemon:
<http://www.monnet-project.eu/lemon#>
PREFIX lexinfo:
<http://lexinfo.net/ontology/2.0/
lexinfo#>
select ?wordForm1 ?language1
?wordForm2 ?language2 ?wordForm3
?language3
WHERE
{GRAPH
<http://quanthistling.info/lod/>
{?word1 a lemon:LexicalForm;
lemon:writtenRep ?wordForm1.
?entry1 lemon:form ?word1;
lemon:sense ?sense1.
?language1 lemon:entry ?entry1.
?sense1 lexinfo:translation ?sense2.
?word2 a lemon:LexicalForm;
lemon:writtenRep ?wordForm2.
?entry2 lemon:form ?word2;
lemon:sense ?sense2.
?language2 lemon:entry ?entry2.
?sense2 lexinfo:translation ?sense3.
?word3 a lemon:LexicalForm;
lemon:writtenRep ?wordForm3.
?entry3 lemon:form ?word3;
lemon:sense ?sense3.
?language3 lemon:entry ?entry3.
FILTER (str(?wordForm1)="casa")
}
}
```

Of course this query can be easily extended to in-

[8] http://lingpy.org/

[9] http://qhanthistling.info/lod/

[10] Note that the filter in this query is computationally expensive and at the moment certain queries may time out as we try and increase server capacity.

corporate entire wordlists, such as the Swadesh list (Swadesh, 1952) or Leipzig-Jakarta list (Tadmor et al., 2010).

Again we emphasize that the combination of disparate data from many dictionaries and lexicons is a first step in a computational historical linguistics pipeline: the results are given in the source documents' orthographic representations and therefore they must be normalized into an interlingual pivot, such as the International Phonetic Alphabet, if phonetic or phonemic analysis is to be applied to the data. This would be the next step before producing phonetic alignments and cognate judgements based on metrics and algorithms for calculating lexical similarity.

## 4 Conclusion

From data being digitized and extracted from print resources, we are creating machine-readable lexicons that are both interoperable with each other (we link semantic senses using the Lemon ontology model) and with other linguistics sources (we use standard language code URIs used by other Linked Data resources in the LLOD).

Future work may proceed in a number of directions, such as:

- building algorithms that identify semantically similar translation-pairs from terse translations, e.g. identify that doculect translations like "coarsely grind", "grind up, crush well", "grind lightly (chili pepper, millet for a quick snack)", "grind lightly (groundnuts) with stones" for different languages can be mapped to a simpler form such as "to crush/grind" for initial comparative analysis

- using NLP Interchange Format (Hellmann et al., 2012) to keep track of where information in the dictionaries comes from – or in other words, use NIF combined with Lemon to annotate the QHL data sources for provenance

- linking to other resources that contain other linguistic and non-linguistic information (e.g. typological data and geographic variables that provide useful information for determining the genealogical and geographical relatedness of languages)

## References


Alexandre Bouchard-Côté, David Hall, Thomas L. Griffiths, and Dan Klein. 2013. Automated reconstruction of ancient languages using probabilistic models of sound change. *PNAS*, 110(11):4224–4229.

R. Bouckaert, P. Lemey, M. Dunn, S. J. Greenhill, A. V. Alekseyenko, A. J. Drummond, R. D. Gray, M. A. Suchard, and Q. D. Atkinson. 2012. Mapping the origins and expansion of the Indo-European language family. *Science*, 337(6097):957–960, Aug.

Gerard de Melo. Submittied. Lexvo.org: Language-related information for the linguistic linked data cloud. *Semantic Web Journal*.

Gil Francopoulo, Monte George, Nicoletta Calzolari, Monica Monachini, Nuria Bel, Mandy Pet, Claudia Soria, et al. 2006. Lexical markup framework (lmf). In *In Proceedings of the Fifth International Conference on Language Resources and Evaluation (LREC 2006)*.

Sebastian Hellmann, Jens Lehmann, and Sören Auer. 2012. Linked-data aware uri schemes for referencing text fragments. In *Knowledge Engineering and Knowledge Management*, pages 175–184. Springer.

Eric. W. Holman, Cecil H. Brown, Søren Wichmann, André Müller, Viveka Velupillai, Harald Hammarström, Sebastian Sauppe, Hagen Jung, Dik Bakker, Pamela Brown, Oleg Belyaev, Matthias Urban, Robert Mailhammer, Johann-Mattis List, and Dimitry Egorov. 2011. Automated dating of the world's language families based on lexical similarity. *Current Anthropology*, 52(6):841–875.

Nancy Ide and Keith Suderman. 2007. Graf: A graph-based format for linguistic annotations. In *Proceedings of the Linguistic Annotation Workshop*, pages 1–8. Association for Computational Linguistics.

Marc Kemps-Snijders, Menzo Windhouwer, Peter Wittenburg, and Sue Ellen Wright. 2008. Isocat: Corralling data categories in the wild. In *LREC*.

Brett Kessler. 2001. *The significance of word lists*. CSLI Publications, Stanford.

Grzegorz Kondrak. 2000. A new algorithm for the alignment of phonetic sequences. In *Proceedings of the 1st North American chapter of the Association for Computational Linguistics conference*, NAACL 2000, pages 288–295, Stroudsburg, PA, USA. Association for Computational Linguistics.

Johann-Mattis List and Steven Moran. 2013. An open source toolkit for quantitative historical linguistics. In *Proceedings of the Association for Computational Linguistics*.

John McCrae, Guadalupe Aguado-de Cea, Paul Buitelaar, Philipp Cimiano, Thierry Declerck, Asunción Gómez Pérez, Jorge Gracia, Laura

Hollink, Elena Montiel-Ponsoda, Dennis Spohr, and Tobias Wunner. 2010. The lemon cookbook. Technical report, CITEC, Universität Bielefeld.

John McCrae, Dennis Spohr, and Philipp Cimiano. 2011. Linking lexical resources and ontologies on the semantic web with lemon. In *The Semantic Web: Research and Applications*, pages 245–259. Springer.

Shijulal Nelson-Sathi, Johann-Mattis List, Hans Geisler, Heiner Fangerau, Russell D. Gray, William Martin, and Tal Dagan. 2011. Networks uncover hidden lexical borrowing in Indo-European language evolution. *Proceedings of the Royal Society B*, 278(1713):1794–1803.

Jelena Prokić, Martijn Wieling, and John Nerbonne. 2009. Multiple sequence alignments in linguistics. In *Proceedings of the EACL 2009 Workshop on Language Technology and Resources for Cultural Heritage, Social Sciences, Humanities, and Education*, pages 18–25, Stroudsburg, PA. Association for Computational Linguistics.

Laurent Romary. 2010. Standardization of the formal representation of lexical information for nlp. *Dictionaries. An International Encyclopedia of Lexicography. Supplementary volume: Recent developments with special focus on computational lexicography.*

Lydia Steiner, Peter F. Stadler, and Michael Cysouw. 2011. A pipeline for computational historical linguistics. *Language Dynamics and Change*, 1(1):89–127.

Morris Swadesh. 1952. Lexico-statistic dating of prehistoric ethnic contacts. *Proceedings of the American Philosophical Society*, 96(4):452–463.

Uri Tadmor, Martin Haspelmath, and Bradley Taylor. 2010. Borrowability and the notion of basic vocabulary. *Diachronica*, 27(2):226–246.

Peter Turchin, Ilja Peiros, and Murray Gell-Mann. 2010. Analyzing genetic connections between languages by matching consonant classes. *Journal of Language Relationship*, 3:117–126.

# Transforming the Data Transcription and Analysis Tool Metadata and Labels into a Linguistic Linked Open Data Cloud Resource

**Antonio Pareja-Lora**
Univ. Complutense de Madrid
Facultad de Informática
28040 – Madrid, Spain
apareja@sip.ucm.es

**María Blume**
Univ. of Texas at El Paso
Dept. of Languages and Linguistics
Liberal Arts Bldg., Room 232
El Paso, Texas 79968
mblume@utep.edu

**Barbara Lust**
Cornell University
Dept. of Human Development
G57 Martha Van Rensselaer
Hall, Ithaca, NY 14853
bcl4@cornell.edu

## Abstract

Developing language resources requires much time, funding and effort. This is why they need to be reused in new projects and developments, so that they may both serve a wider scientific community and sustain their cost. The main problems that prevent this from happening are that (1) language resources are rarely free and/or easy to locate; and (2) they are hardly ever interoperable. Therefore, the language resource community is now working to transform their most valuable assets into open and interoperable resources, which can then be shared and linked with other open and interoperable resources. This will allow data to be reanalyzed and repurposed. In this paper, we present the first steps taken to transform a set of such resources, namely the Data Transcription and Analysis Tool's (DTA) metadata and data, into an open and interoperable language resource. These first steps include the development of two ontologies that formalize the conceptual model underlying the DTA metadata and the labels used in the DTA to annotate both utterances and their transcriptions at several annotation levels.

## 1 Introduction

As the web evolves into the Web 2.0 and is complemented by the Web 3.0,[1] the Semantic Web and/or the Web of Data (Auer and Hellmann, 2012), the need for language resources to be transformed into open, sharable and interoperable resources becomes more urgent. Lately, this transformation has been achieved by converting language resources into linked open data sets and/or graphs. These linked data help formalize and make explicit common-sense knowledge in a way that satisfies the needs of the Web 3.0, the Semantic Web and/or the Web of Data. Indeed, computers are already using these linked data to process information "more intelligently".

In this context, many language resources may unfortunately be left aside and fade into oblivion if they fail to address this challenge (which would entail a waste of considerable data and effort for the scientific community). Making language resources easier to share and more interoperable would help researchers collaborate and build on others' work.

This is the case of the resources generated by the Data Transcription and Analysis Tool (DTA).[2] The DTA tool is a primary research web application that organizes metadata and data primarily for the study of language acquisition, either monolingual or multilingual.[3] Henceforth, we will use the term DTA to refer to the tool itself, its experiment bank component, and its associated corpora. The DTA allows for long distance collaborative research and serves as a teaching tool for training students on language data management and analysis. Besides providing a powerful relational database, which handles both experimental and naturalistic data, it also structures the primary data creation process from its initial stages. Hence, the DTA represents data so that it can be analyzed subsequently in a standardized and theory-neutral way, which ensures data comparability within a language and across languages. At the same time, it allows researchers to create project-specific codings, allowing multiple types of analyses in their own data or linking data across projects. This tool was created as part of the VCLA's[4] Virtual Linguistics Lab[5] to take advantage of the opportunities

[1] http://en.wikipedia.org/wiki/Web_2.0#Web_3.0

[2] http://webdta.clal.cornell.edu

[3] Access to the DTA cybertool is password protected due to Human Subjects confidentiality requirements and the intellectual property rights of the contributing researchers. To allow for wider dissemination, multiple levels of access must be set. The PIs are currently investigating potential funding sources for this dissemination.

[4] http://vcla.clal.cornell.edu/

[5] http://clal.cornell.edu/vll/

the digital age created for the interdisciplinary, cross-linguistic study of language acquisition (Blume and Lust, 2012; Blume et al., 2012).[6]

The research presented here is the result of a joint work in which we compared and linked two different language resources, namely OntoLingAnnot's ontologies (Pareja-Lora and Aguado de Cea, 2010; Pareja-Lora, 2012a; Pareja-Lora 2012b; Pareja-Lora, 2013) and the Data Transcription and Analysis Tool (Blume and Lust, 2012; Blume et al., 2012).

In this paper we introduce (i) the metadata and the labels that are used within the DTA to annotate data on language acquisition; and (ii) the two ontologies that we have now built to represent, respectively, the DTA metadata and the DTA labels. In some cases, these labels (such as Noun Phrase, Sentence, Statement, Question or Answer) can be linked to ISOCat categories (Windhouwer and Wright, 2012) and/or are equivalent to some GOLD element (Farrar and Langendoen, 2010).[7] These links and equivalences are being included in the ontologies as well, which should help add the DTA ontologies to the Linguistic Linked Open Data (LLOD) cloud[8] (Chiarcos et al., 2012) shortly.

Our paper is organized as follows. The DTA metadata categories are presented in section 2. Section 3 introduces the labels used in the DTA to annotate the data linguistically. A comparison of the DTA labels and metadata with those of other related projects, such as CHILDES and the Language Archive (LA), is provided in section 4. In Section 5, we show the two ontologies built to conceptualize, the DTA metadata and the DTA labels, each one in a dedicated subsection. Finally, section 6 discusses the conclusions of this research and gives an overview of our future work.

## 2 The DTA metadata categories

The DTA is based on 10 tables with the following basic markup categories: project, dataset, subject, session, recording, transcription, utterance, coding set, coding, and utterance coding. Metadata codings involve the project and subject levels and the dataset level leading to transcribed utterances and related linguistic codings. In the DTA the data are organized in *projects*. A project contains several *subjects*. Each subject is a participant whose language is studied in the project. The subject screen is where all the participant info is stored. The application uses the UTF-8 encoding to store text and adopts the ISO 639-3 standard language codes, which cover over 7000 languages. It links with GeoNames.org for geographic reference.

Each project contains the following main sections of information: Project Main Info, References, Subjects, Datasets, Coding, and Queries.

### 2.1 The Project Main Info Section

Under *Project Main Info* there are three tabs: *Main Info, Results, Summary and Discussion. Main info* provides an overview of the main information on a project so that other users may decide whether they choose to continue reading about this project or move to another one. The text fields include title (project's name), principal investigator, additional and assisting investigators, acknowledgments, dates, purpose, leading hypotheses, and comments. *Results* and *summary and discussion* allow one to enter the results and the discussion for the whole project (from all the datasets).

### 2.2 The References Section

*References* include *publications*, *presentations*, *related studies*, and *references*. They all have the same basic structure based on an APA format. The only variation is on the items one can select under "type". Under *publications, related studies, and references,* "type" includes book, chapter, article, web page, thesis, dissertation, and other. All types include the basic fields title, authors, and date, and other needed fields according to the reference type. *Presentations* contains the following types: conference, invited speaker, colloquium, and other (which are also included under *related studies*) with the same basic fields as publications plus "place of publication/presentation", "URL" and "notes".

### 2.3 The Subjects Section

The subject data are not session-specific; i.e., permanent characteristics of the subject are recorded in this screen. The subject screen has two sections: *Subject* and *Caretakers*. *Subject* in-

[6] The DTA capabilities extend to other areas of language knowledge and use, such as language deterioration in adult dementia. Although the VLL and its cybertools were created with the study of language acquisition and multilingualism in mind, they can not only be expanded to other language areas but also used as a prototype for data management and linking in other areas of scientific investigation

[7] The cross-linguistic data in the DTA should also be a good test for how well GOLD categories work across languages, an issue central to the 2005 E-Meld workshop (*cf.* http://www.emeld.org/workshop/2005/).

[8] http://linguistics.okfn.org/resources/llod/

cludes ID, name, gender, DOB, nationality, ethnicity, place of birth, whether the subject has any language or cognitive impairment, whether Human Subjects required documents have been filled in and a multilingualism questionnaire has been completed, the subject's contact information, and comments. Information on the language(s), dialect(s), and levels of language comprehension and production for each language are also indicated. When subjects are children, information on their caretakers is also stored including relationship with the subject, occupation, name, contact information, languages, dialects, and levels of proficiency.

### 2.4 The Sessions and Datasets Section

The subjects participate in different recording sessions (tests, observations, or surveys). The sessions are organized in groups called *datasets*. Each subject has at least one session, but they can have more than one. All sessions for a subject may be part of one dataset but they can be divided into more datasets.[9] Each dataset contains the recordings, transcriptions, and codings for each session.

Datasets contain two main sections: *Main Info* and *Sessions*. *Main Info* includes title, type (investigation or experiment), topic, abstract, and related WebDTA project/datasets, hypotheses, subjects (a summary description of subjects in the dataset), methods (production, comprehension, perceptual discrimination, or grammaticality judgment), design (factors, variables, conditions, controls, specific hypotheses, statistical analyses), stimuli, procedures, scoring, results, and conclusions. *Sessions* include the following information fields: Session ID, date, interviewer, assistants, session length, task, languages used, and session location. Information on the subject characteristics at each particular session is also included: Current age (calculated by the DTA), number of siblings, position among siblings, address, length of residence, education, occupation, and school. Fundamental information (name and transcription identifier) on the session participants besides the subject and interviewer is also created. Information on the general activities carried out during the session and the analyses performed on the data are included.

[9] Each project user can determine what constitutes a dataset; they are usually divided in terms of the experimental task used (each different task used in one project constitutes an independent dataset) or by participant characteristics (e.g. Spanish-speakers vs. English-speakers).

## 3 The DTA Labels

Labels in the DTA are called *codings*. Codings and their related queries can be established at a global level or at an individual dataset level. Global codings can be used by all projects and can only be established by users with administrator access. Codings are grouped in coding sets. Simple coding sets were created to standardize and calibrate basic levels of linguistic analysis. They may also introduce students to linguistic coding with increasing levels of analysis/difficulty. Experimental projects create their project-specific coding sets in addition to basic ones, as do researchers who work with natural speech.

There are three basic coding sets: *Utterance transcription*, *speech act*, and *basic linguistic*. *Utterance transcription* includes text fields that give information to contextualize the utterances[10] and allows one to add simple linguistic descriptions, translations and glosses of non-English utterances.[11] *Speech act* lists common speech acts with some additional ones common in child data[12] and asks about the spontaneous or responsive character of the utterance, and therefore relates more to the pragmatic/discursive aspects of the data.[13] Finally, *basic linguistic* asks whether the utterance is a sentence or not, and whether the sentence has an overt verb,[14] as well as for the number of morphemes, words, and syllables of the utterance, to calculate the Mean Length of Utterance (MLU), an important developmental measure in child language acquisition. Additional basic linguistic codings are now being created.

[10] *General context* (a description of the participants, their location and activities throughout the session), *utterance context* (the context necessary to understand the contents of a particular utterance, for example, what the speaker is referring to or who they are addressing), and *comments*.

[11] *Morphological coding*, *word-by-word gloss, general gloss* (a translation into English that conveys the meaning of the utterance regardless of structure), and *phonetic transcription*.

[12] Declarative/assertive, question, imperative, promise, wish/request, expressives/exclamations, yes/no/OK, naming, counting, singing, politeness, greetings, unclear, and other.

[13] Spontaneous, self-repetition, other repetition, answer-Y/N, answer-Wh, other answer (i.e., when the subject answers a question which is not a Wh-question or a Y/N-question), unclear, other.

[14] Verbless sentences are common in early child speech (e.g. *Me [ə] cookie from mommy*). The corresponding labels are "is this a sentence?" and "is the verb overt?".

## 4 Comparing the DTA with other systems

Certain databases, such as CHILDES and the Language Archive, share some of the purposes of the DTA. Given that both CHILDES and DTA have focused on child language data, they obviously have common or similar labels in the codings that they adopt (about 24[15]). However, one main difference is that the DTA provides the user with a structured interface for primary data entry and management, while CHILDES lists possible metadata fields in its accompanying manual, and provides no structure for the researcher. The information on what to fill in when archiving data is provided in the CHILDES manual in a narrative form.[16]

One label in CHILDES may be covered by more than one label in the DTA. For example, the "creator" label corresponds to three labels in the DTA, namely "Principal Investigator", "Additional Investigators", and "Assisting investigators." A "How was data collected" label is covered by the DTA's more specific fields under the Dataset Main Info: "type, method type, method details, design, and stimuli". Some identical labels refer to different things.[17] CHILDES asks for information on the funding for the project which is not included in the DTA, but could easily be incorporated, and on some other aspects which the DTA creators did not consider relevant, e.g., "religion", "interests", "friends", "layout of child's home and bedroom" and whatever is included under "and so forth".

Although researcher compliance in filling the required fields cannot be assured, the main advantage of the DTA is its structured format, which helps researchers in the primary data creation process.[18]

To compare the DTA and the Language Archive (LA), we looked at the metadata fields in Brugman et al. (2003). For clarification of the LA field definitions we consulted IMDI Metadata 3.0.4. The DTA and the LA share many of their fields since both have language archiving and metadata creation purposes in mind. The main differences are related to content organization. While the LA organizes data in terms of sessions, with project information contained inside a session and no dataset level, the DTA organizes it in terms of projects that contain datasets which in turn contain sessions.[19]

The main differences between the systems stem from their partially divergent purposes. The DTA was developed mainly for child language acquisition so it asks for detailed information on the child's caretakers and it was intended for experimental as well as observational data; thus it has much more detailed fields related to project and dataset experimental design (19) which do not exist in the LA. The LA has a much more detailed information section on the different types of resources (it distinguishes "source", "resource", and "written resource" with detailed information for type, format, encoding, access, and anonymity for all), and on the type of communication context and genre of the interaction (30), some of which would be relevant for the DTA. Surprisingly, there are more than a few fields that the DTA has which are not child/experiment specific which the LA does not have, such as the participant's length of residence at the session location, date of birth, nationality, place of birth, levels of language or cognitive impairment, dialect, whether he/she is a native speaker of the language used in the session, and his/her levels of proficiency in the language. The DTA also has a more detailed division of references as explained in section 2.2 above.

[15] Numbers in parentheses refer to number of fields.

[16] "**7. Biographical data.** Where possible, extensive demographic, dialectological, and psychometric data should be provided for each informant. There should be information on topics such as age, gender, siblings, schooling, social class, occupation, previous residences, religion, interests, friends, and so forth.[…]" (MacWhinney, 2012: 23)

[17] E.g. "acknowledgments" in the DTA refers to acknowledgments of the persons who made the project possible, and in CHILDES it refers to the rules for citing data used by a researcher who did not create such data.

[18] In CHILDES, the requested information is not completed in several of the available corpora. To take one relevant case, the CHILDES corpus does not have all the requested information and includes several pieces of information (related to OLAC and IMDI), which are not mentioned in the manual. To get more complete information on a corpus, readers are directed to the Database Manuals in which each corpus is described. Length of descriptions varies from a short paragraph to two or three pages.

[19] The DTA and the LA share very few fields at the different levels (i.e., project description (3), session description (4) and transcription/annotation (1)). Several fields have similar names in the two systems (20). Nine fields in the LA are divided into more than one field in the DTA (e.g., *task* in the LA corresponds to *dataset method type, dataset method details,* and *session task* in the DTA, *annotator* in the LA corresponds to *transcriber* and *checker* in the DTA).

## 5 Ontological Formalization of DTA Categories

As shown in the previous section, the DTA provides the most detailed and exhaustive repertoire developed so far with metadata and labels for child language analysis and annotation. Therefore, it seems reasonable to formalize this repertoire by means of some ontologies. This formalization will help to compare, integrate and link DTA annotations with the annotations resulting from CHILDES or the LA later on.[20]

As noted above, the DTA language acquisition data are annotated with extensive metadata, such as the time and place where they were collected, and the data (e.g. transcriptions) are annotated linguistically. At this time, these linguistic annotations pertain mostly to the pragmatic and the phonological levels, in order to calibrate incoming data, but also, to a lesser extent, to the morphosyntactic and the syntactic levels.

Thus, the first ontology built for DTA (namely the DTA Metadata Ontology) contains a formalization of the DTA metadata, which is particular of this initiative and, hence, had to be built mostly from scratch. The second ontology (that is, the DTA Labels Ontology) includes a conceptualization of the labels used to annotate DTA transcriptions linguistically. Accordingly, it reuses other linguistic resources and ontologies. In particular, the OntoLingAnnot set of ontologies (Pareja-Lora and Aguado de Cea, 2010; Pareja-Lora, 2012a; Pareja-Lora 2012b; Pareja-Lora, 2013) has been reused to formalize the DTA pragmatic level labels, [21] including convenient links to ISOCat[22] categories and OWL equivalences with GOLD elements. This will help make the DTA ontologies become part of the Linguistic Linked Open Data (LLOD) cloud. Each of the ontologies is described below.

### 5.1 The DTA Metadata Ontology

The DTA Metadata Ontology contains the different elements described in section 2. In its development, we have followed as faithfully as possible the categorizations applied in developing the DTA. The top-level classes of this ontology are shown in Figure 1.

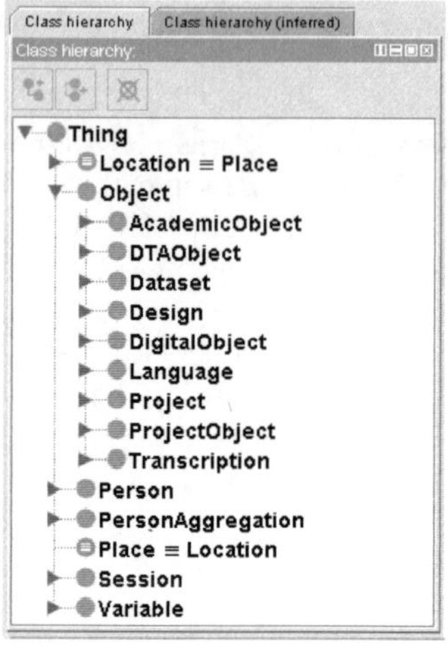

Figure 1: DTA Metadata Ontology – Main classes

These top-level classes include the formalization of some of the ten DTA basic categories presented in section 2 (namely `Project`, `Dataset`, `Session` and `Transcription`). The ones not shown in the figure are subclasses of one or several of the classes shown: `Subject` is `rdfs:subClassOf Person`; the classes formalizing recording, coding and coding set are subclasses of `DTAObject` and of `ProjectObject`; and `Utterance` and `UtteranceCoding` have been included in the DTA Labels Ontology (cf., next section). Other relevant items in the DTA, i.e. languages, are also represented at this level, by means of the class `Language`.

The `Project` and `ProjectObject` classes have two main subclasses respectively, i.e., `DTAProject` and `DTAProjectObject`. They are the most prominent subclasses of this ontology, as shown in Figure 2. Indeed, as shown in the figure, most of the concepts presented in sections 2.1-2.4 have been represented as subclasses of these two concepts.

The classes `DTAInformationSection` and `DTAInfoTab` are related by means of the object property `HasPart` in the ontology, that is, `DTAInformationSection HasPart DTAInfoTab`. Thus, each of the tabs associated to the different sections of information have been straightforwardly formalized as subclasses of one of the subclasses of `DTAInfoTab`, namely `ProjectMainInfoTab`, `ReferencesTab`, `SubjectsTab` and `DatasetTab`. They are not exhaustively described here to avoid redundancy with section 2. However, it is important to note that (1) the formalization of the ReferencesTab entailed the inclusion of a whole sub-ontology of academic objects, shown in Figure 3.

[20] The resulting ontologies have been published under a 3-clause BSD license at https://github.com/apareja/DTA_Ontologies.

[21] For more information about OntoLingAnnot (including the code of its ontological modules), please contact the first author of this paper.

[22] http://www.isocat.org

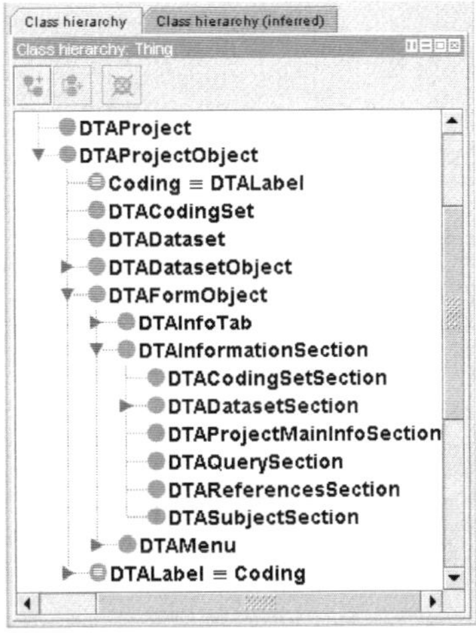


Figure 2: DTA Metadata Ontology – `DTAProjectObject` main subclasses

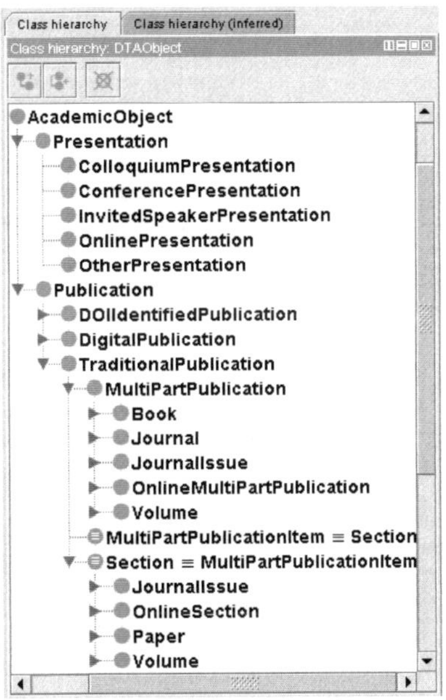


Figure 3: DTA Metadata Ontology – the `AcademicObject` sub-ontology

All these classes have corresponding data properties attached, which represent the different text and menu fields used in DTA to assign values and annotations (*cf.* section 2). The resulting hierarchy of properties is partially shown in Figure 4. Also a number of object properties have been formalized in this ontology, but they are not described due to space limitations.

## 5.2 The DTA Labels Ontology

The DTA Labels Ontology includes the DTA elements discussed in section 3. They are used in the annotation of utterances in the DTA. We decided to develop a separate ontology for these elements due to their more general nature and, hence, their higher reusability in all kinds of linguistic annotation projects.

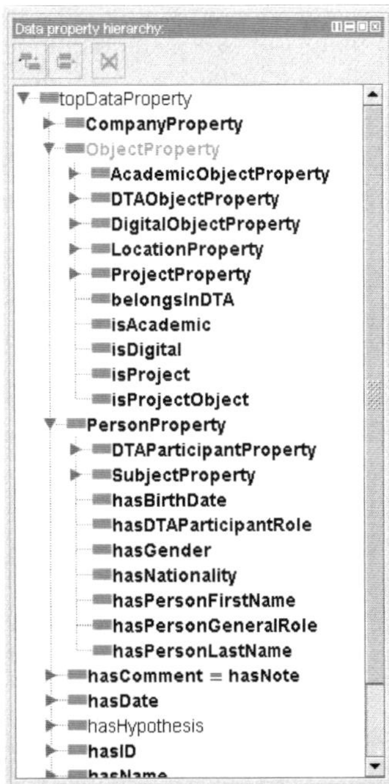


Figure 4: DTA Metadata Ontology – The hierarchy of data properties

In this case, since the DTA labels are a particular case of linguistic annotation, we reused other existing ontologies and repositories of categories for linguistic annotation, such as GOLD, DCR/ISOCat, OntoTag (Aguado de Cea et al., 2002; 2004; Pareja-Lora, 2012c), and OntoLingAnnot. We kept the same **criteria and methodologies of classification and subdivision** applied in these other linguistic resources, making the DTA Labels Ontology more interoperable with them.[23] For example, we developed three separate taxonomies within the ontology, one for linguistic units, one for linguistic attributes (or features), and another one for the linguistic values that these attributes can take. The super-classes of these taxonomies are, respec-

[23] However, the formalization of the links and the equivalences with e.g. GOLD and ISOCat is still ongoing. Whereas GOLD entities are linked by means of `owl:equivalentClass` statements, ISOCat categories are linked by means of an ad-hoc defined data property, namely `correspondsToISOCatDataCategory`, whose value is an `xsd:anyURI` pointer to the category's ISO persistent identifier. A matching between the DTA ontologies with the FOAF (Friend Of A Friend) vocabulary (http://www.foaf-project.org) and with the Dublin Core Metadata (http://dublincore.org/) is planned as well. All the matches found will be added subsequently to the DTA ontologies.

tively, LinguisticUnit, LinguisticAttribute and Linguistic-Value, which have been imported from the OntoLingAnnot ontologies.

Each of these taxonomies is linked to each other by the corresponding relation of the OntoLingAnnot model, namely: LinguisticUnit **hasFeature** LinguisticAttribute, LinguisticAttribute **takesValue** LinguisticValue, LinguisticValue **isValueTakenBy** LinguisticAttribute, LinguisticAttribute **isAttachedTo** LinguisticUnit.

We created a **DTALabel class**, which is a rdfs:subClassOf LinguisticAttribute. Most DTA labels are subclasses of DTALabel. We have only classified DTA glosses differently, since they are in fact the aggregation of a label (namely WordByWordGlossLabel or GeneralGlossLabel, which are the subclasses of DTAGlossLabel – see below) and a value (the actual text provided as a gloss).

Each DTALabel is a GlobalCoding or a ProjectSpecificCoding. The main **subclasses of GlobalCoding** are BasicLinguisticLabel (which has only one subclass, i.e. DTASyntacticLabel), UtteranceTranscriptionLabel (whose subclasses are Context, DTAGlossLabel, MorphologicalCodingLabel and PhoneticTranscriptionLabel) and SpeechActLabel, whose subclasses detail the attributes that can be applied to Searle's types of speech acts (luo:Assertive,[24] luo:Commissive, luo:Declaration, luo:Directive and luo:Expressive[25]) and have been classified accordingly.

The main **subclasses of ProjectSpecificCoding** are isAdjectivalPhrase, isAdverbialPhrase, isFragment, isNounPhrase, isPrepositionalPhase, isRelativePronoun, isSentence and isWh-Word.

The **linguistic units included and/or imported into the DTA Labels Ontology** are the following: luo:PhonologicalUnit (whose main subclasses are luo:Phoneme, luo:ProsodicUnit, luo:Syllable and luo:Utterance), luo:MorphoSyntacticUnit (whose main subclasses are luo:MorphologicalUnit, luo:SyntacticUnit and luo:Word), luo:SemanticUnit, luo:DiscourseUnit, luo:PragmaticUnit (which is one of the superclasses of luo:SpeechAct in this ontology, together with luo:SpeechUnit), and luo:TextUnit (whose main subclasses relevant to DTA, are MorphologicalCoding, PhoneticTranscription, PhoneticTranscriptionSymbol, UtteranceTranscription and luo:Text).

We have also imported the luo:Morpheme class, which is an rdfs:subClassOf luo:MorphologicalUnit, and several subclasses of luo:SyntacticUnit, such as luo:Clause, luo:Phrase (and some of its subclasses, i.e. luo:AdjectivalPhrase, luo:AdverbialPhrase, luo:NounPhrase and luo:PrepositionalPhrase) and Sentence (together with some of its subclasses, i.e., ComplexSentence, CompoundSentence and SimpleSentence). We have also added a particular DTA rdfs:subClassOf luo:SyntacticUnit (Fragment), which represents the syntactic projection of those transcribed utterances that cannot be considered an instance of any of the other syntactic units.

The main **individuals** of the DTA Labels Ontology are members of the subclasses of SpeechActLabel; for example, CountingLabel, GreetingLabel, NamingLabel, PolitenessLabel, SingingLabel, PromiseLabel, QuestionLabel and YesOrNoOrOKLabel formalize the particular types of speech act labels available within the DTA (see footnotes 12 and 13). They are used for the subclassification and/or annotation of utterances as speech acts, for instance.

Briefly, the DTA Label Ontology entities were categorized as LinguisticUnit, LinguisticAttribute or LinguisticValue subclasses or individuals, and they were also linked among them with suitable **object properties**, such as Has/PartOf, Labels/isLabelledWith, hasSyntacticProjection/isSyntacticProjectionOf, or hasTranscription/isTranscriptionOf. As shown in these examples, we declared an inverse property for each direct object property identified, in order to facilitate inferences.

Overall, the most relevant characteristic of this categorization is that it allows for a formalization of DTA annotations as linguistic RDF triples, as in the OntoLingAnnot model. This will allow for

[24] The luo namespace stands for OntoTag's and OntoLingAnnot's Linguistic Unit Ontology (LUO).

[25] This classes are subclasses of luo:SpeechAct, see below.

a fairly straightforward conversion of DTA annotations into RDF triples and, therefore, into linked (open) data. Some statistics about the number of classes, properties, data types, individuals and axioms included in these ontologies have been included in Table 1.

Table 1: Some statistic about the elements included in the DTA ontologies

| DTA Ontologies Statistics | DTA Metadata Ontology | DTA Labels Ontology |
|---|---|---|
| **Classes** | 169 | 137 |
| **Object properties** | 139 | 12 |
| **Data properties** | 188 | 9 |
| **Annot. properties** | 61 | 5 |
| **Datatypes** | 32 | 7 |
| **Individuals** | 2 | 66 |
| **Axioms** | 2222 | 698 |
| **Logical axioms** | 1406 | 350 |
| **Subclass axioms** | 486 | 193 |

## 6 Summary and future work

In this paper, we have presented the first steps in the transformation of the DTA metadata and labels into a Linguistic Linked Open Data resource. The main results of this work are the two ontologies presented in Section 5, which formalize the DTA elements, described in Sections 2 and 3. We have also provided a comparison in Section 4 that shows that this is, to the best of our knowledge, one of the most relevant and detailed initiatives in the study and annotation of child language.

A suitable integration and linking of DTA annotations with the annotations resulting from CHILDES or the LA is still pending. This would first require the formalization of the label mappings between DTA and CHILDES and the LA (already identified in Section 4) in the two ontologies presented here.

Other future work might include a re-engineering of the DTA to convert it into a semantic portal, using Semantic Web technologies. This would allow us to produce automatically open linked data annotations in the future, instead of (1) storing the annotations first in a database; and then (2) transforming them into linked data.

Even though it is in its initial stages, this collaboration has already produced two immediate outcomes: (i) the evaluation of the categories included in OntoLingAnnot's ontologies against the resources in the DTA[26] and (ii) the detection of inconsistencies and gaps in the annotations of linguistic elements in the DTA, with the definitions in other linguistic resources.[27] This two-way evaluation follows an interdisciplinary approach (computational and linguistic) and will allow for the transformation of the existing DTA data into linked (open) data, using the items now formalized in the DTA Metadata Ontology and the DTA Labels Ontology, allowing future linked-data-based, data-intensive research. Moreover, since the OntoLingAnnot model is ISO conformant and aims at the interoperability of linguistic resources and annotations, it will lead to the standardization of the DTA in order to make it more interoperable.

## Acknowledgments

The authors thank the organizing committee of the first Linked Data in Linguistics workshop for helping us know of each other's projects and therefore initiate this collaboration. We also thank the anonymous reviewers for their many useful suggestions for this paper.

The DTA project was supported by several funding sources: "Transforming the Primary Research Process through Cybertool Dissemination: "An Implementation of a Virtual Center for the Study of Language Acquisition", National Science Foundation grant to María Blume and Barbara Lust, 2008, NSF OCI-0753415; "Planning Grant: A Virtual Center for Child Language Acquisition Research", National Science Foundation grant to Barbara Lust, 2003, NSF BCS-0126546; "Planning Information Infrastructure Through a New Library-Research Partnership", National Science Foundation Small Grant for Exploratory Research to Janet McCue and Barbara Lust, 2004-2006; Cornell University Faculty Innovation in Teaching Awards, Cornell Institute for Social and Economic Research (CISER); New York State Hatch grant; Grant Number T32 DC00038 from the National Institute on Deafness and Other Communication Disorders (NIDCD).

[26] For example, the inclusion of `rdfs:subClassOf luo:SyntacticUnit (Fragment)`; *cf.* section 5 and, in particular, Figure 3.

[27] For example, the DTA classifies sentences according to their structure into two types: complex and simple; and then subdivides complex sentences into those involving coordination and those involving subordination. This classification does not correspond to how sources such as the SIL Glossary (http://www-01.sil.org/linguistics/GlossaryOflinguisticTerms/) or OntoTag and OntoLingAnnot classify them. In these other resources, (1) complex sentence refers to sentences including at least one main clause and at least one subordinate clause; and (2) compound sentence refers to sentences that consist of two or more coordinate clauses.

We gratefully acknowledge the collaboration of the Virtual Center for Language Acquisition's other founding members: Suzanne Flynn (MIT), Claire Foley (Boston College), Marianella Casasola, Claire Cardie, James Gair, and Qi Wang (Cornell University); Elise Temple (NeuroFocus); Liliana Sánchez (Rutgers University at New Brusnwick); Jennifer Austin (Rutgers University at Newark); YuChin Chien (California State University at San Bernardino); and Usha Lakshmanan (Southern Illinois University at Carbondale). We are grateful for the collaboration of scholars who are VCLA affiliates including Sujin Yang (Korea), Gita Martohardjono, Valerie Shafer, and Isabelle Barrière (City University of New York); Cristina Dye (Newcastle University); Yarden Kedar, (the Center for Academic Sudies, Israel), Joy Hirsch (Columbia University); Ellen Courtney and Alfredo Urzúa (University of Texas at El Paso); Sarah Callahan (University of California at San Diego); Jorge Iván Pérez Silva (Pontificia Universidad Católica Del Perú), Kwee Ock Lee (Kyungsung University); R. Amritavalli (Central Institute of English and Foreign Languages); A. Usha Rani (Osmania University).

We thank application developers Ted Caldwell and Greg Kops (GORGES); consultants Cliff Crawford and Tommy Cusick; student research assistants Darlin Alberto, Gabriel Clandorf, Natalia Buitrago, Poornima Guna, Jennie Lin, Marina Kalashnikova, Martha Rayas Tanaka, Lizzeth Jensen, María Jiménez, and Mónica Martínez; and the many students at all the participating institutions who helped us with comments and suggestions. In particular, we thank Janet McCue of Cornell University Library and her collaborators at Cornell A. Mann Library for their assistance on integration of metadata standards and structure to our emerging DTA tool and their assistance in developing formal relations between research labs and University Libraries.

## References

Guadalupe Aguado de Cea, Asunción Gómez-Pérez, Inmaculada Álvarez de Mon, Antonio Pareja-Lora, and Rosario Plaza-Arteche. 2002. OntoTag: A semantic web page linguistic annotation model. In *Semantic Web Meets Language Resources*. AAAI Technical Report WS-02-16, pp. 20–29. Menlo Park, California, USA, 2002. AAAI Press.

Guadalupe Aguado de Cea, Asunción Gómez-Pérez, Inmaculada Álvarez de Mon, Antonio Pareja-Lora. 2004. OntoTag's linguistic ontologies: Improving semantic web annotations for a better language understanding in machines. In *Proceedings of the International Conference on Information Technology: Coding and Computing (ITCC'04)*, vol. 2, pp. 124–128, Washington, DC, USA, 2004. IEEE Computer Society.

Sören Auer and Sebastian Hellmann. The Web of Data: Decentralized, collaborative, interlinked and interoperable In *Proceedings of the 8th International Conference on Language Resources and Evaluation (LREC-2012)*, Istanbul, Turkey, May 2012.

María Blume and Barbara Lust. 2012. First steps in transforming the primary research process through a Virtual Linguistic Lab for the study of language acquisition and use: Challenges and accomplishments. *Journal of Computational Science Education*, vol. 3 (1): 34-46.

María Blume, Suzanne, Flynn, and Barbara Lust. 2012. Creating linked data for the interdisciplinary international collaborative study of language acquisition and use: Achievements and challenges of a new Virtual Linguistics Lab. In Christian Chiarcos, Sebastian Nordhoff, and Sebastian Hellmann (eds.) *Linked Data in Linguistics. Representing and Connecting Language Data and Language Metadata*, pp. 85-96. Heidelberg: Springer.

Hennie Brugman, Daan Broeder, and Gunter Senft. 2003. Documentation of language and archiving of language data at the Max Planck Institute for Psycholinguistics in Nijmegen. Paper presented at the *Ringvorlesung "Bedrohte Sprachen" Sprachenwert – Dokumentation – Revitalisierung*. Fakultät für Linguistik und Literaturwissenschaft. Universität Bielefeld. 05/02/2003. [http://www.mpi.nl/IMDI/documents/articles/BI-EL-PaperA2.pdf]

Christian Chiarcos, Sebastian Hellmann and Sebastian Nordhoff. 2012. Linking linguistic resources: Examples from the Open Linguistics Working Group, In Christian Chiarcos, Sebastian Nordhoff and Sebastian Hellmann (eds.) *Linked Data in Linguistics. Representing Language Data and Metadata*, pp. 201-216. Heidelberg: Springer.

Scott Farrar and D. Terence Langendoen. 2010. An OWL-DL implementation of GOLD: An ontology for the Semantic Web. In A. Witt and D. Metzing (eds.) *Linguistic Modeling of Information and Markup Languages*, pp. 45-66. Dordrecht:Springer.

IMDI. 2003. Isle Metadata Initiative (IMDI) Part 1. Metadata elements for session descriptions. Version 3.0.4. October 2003. [http://www.mpi.nl/IMDI/documents/Proposals/IMDI_MetaData_3.0.3.pdf]

Brian MacWhinney. 2012. *The CHILDES Project. Tools for analyzing talk-Electronic edition. Part 1.*

*The CHAT transcription format.* August 6, 2012. [http://childes.psy.cmu.edu/manuals/CHAT.pdf]

Antonio Pareja-Lora. 2012a. OntoLingAnnot's Ontologies: Facilitating Interoperable Linguistic Annotations (Up to the Pragmatic Level). In Christian Chiarcos, Sebastian Nordhoff and Sebastian Hellmann (eds.) *Linked Data in Linguistics. Representing Language Data and Metadata*, pp. 117-127. Heidelberg: Springer.

Antonio Pareja-Lora. 2012b. OntoLingAnnot's LRO: An Ontology of Linguistic Relations. In *Proceedings of the 10th Terminology and Knowledge Engineering Conference (TKE 2012).* Madrid, June 2012, pp. 49-64. [http://www.oeg-upm.net/tke2012/proceedings, paper 04]

Antonio Pareja-Lora. 2012c. *Providing Linked Linguistic and Semantic Web Annotations – The OntoTag Hybrid Annotation Model.* Saarbrücken: LAP – LAMBERT Academic Publishing.

Antonio Pareja-Lora. 2013. The pragmatic level of OntoLingAnnot's ontologies and their use in pragmatic annotation for language teaching. In J. Arús, M.E., Bárcena, and T. Read (eds.) *Languages for Special Purposes in the Digital Era.* Springer [IN PRESS].

Antonio Pareja-Lora and Guadalupe Aguado de Cea. 2010. Modeling Discourse-related terminology in OntoLingAnnot's ontologies. In *Proceedings of the TKE 2010 workshop "Establishing and using ontologies as a basis for terminological and knowledge engineering resources"*. Dublin, August 2010.

Menzo Windhouwer and Sue Ellen Wright. 2012. Linking to linguistic data categories in ISOcat. In Christian Chiarcos, Sebastian Nordhoff and Sebastian Hellmann (eds.) *Linked Data in Linguistics. Representing Language Data and Metadata*, pp. 99–107. Heidelberg: Springer.

# Releasing multimodal data as Linguistic Linked Open Data: An experience report

**Peter Menke**
SFB 673, Project X1
University of Bielefeld

**John McCrae**
CIT-EC
University of Bielefeld

**Philipp Cimiano**
SFB 673, CIT-EC
University of Bielefeld

pmenke@techfak.uni-bielefeld.de
{jmccrae,cimiano}@cit-ec.uni-bielefeld.de

**Abstract**

In this paper we describe an implemented framework for releasing multimodal corpora as Linked Data. In particular, we describe our experiences in releasing a multimodal corpus based on an online chat game as Linked Data. Building on an internal multimodal data model we call FiESTA, we have implemented a library that enhances existing libraries and classes by functionality allowing to convert the data to RDF. Our framework is implemented on the Rails web application framework. We argue that this work can be highly useful for further contributions to the Linked Data community, especially from the fields of spoken dialogue and multimodal communication.

## 1 Introduction

In recent years, many linguistic resources have been released as Linked Data (Chiarcos et al., 2011). Most of the datasets that are part of the so called Linguistic Linked Open Data (LLOD) cloud consist of dictionaries, written corpora or lexica. However, multimodal dataset are currently heavily underrepresented. In order to address this gap, we describe a framework supporting the easy publication of multimodal data as RDF / Linked Data which is based on an existing multimodal data model and on the Rails framework. In this paper we describe our approach and summarize our experiences. In particular, we describe our experiences in releasing a multimodal corpus based on an online chat game as Linked Data. The corpus consists of chats and related actions in an object arrangement game using a computer-mediated setting. It contains multiple forms of annotation, including primary material such as text transcripts and information about object movements as well as secondary analysis such as phrase structure analysis of the text. Due to the challenging nature of the data, in particular that it contains annotations on multiple timelines, we developed a new model for the representation of this data, which we call FiESTA.

In order to express both established and new data categories and properties, from linguistics as well as from nonlinguistic communication, we developed a new data category registry, which contains links to other resources in the LLOD cloud, in particular to the ISOcat data category repository (Windhouwer and Wright, 2012), but also serves as a place where categories from novel research fields (mainly multimodal communication) can be collected, discussed, until they have settled down and are stable enough for an integration into more authoritative category registries, such as ISOcat. By means of this we aim to make the re-

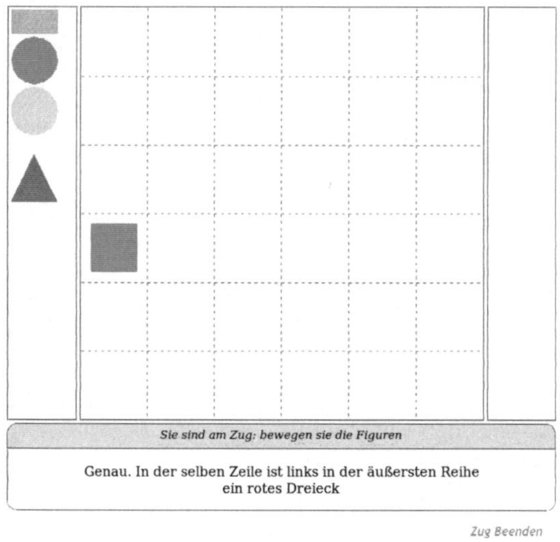


Figure 1: A screen configuration as seen by the *slider*, who can see the last chat message (bottom part) and move objects with a mouse. Unused objects are stored in an area on the left.

source more widely available and to enable a long and successful lifecycle for the resource.

Furthermore, we describe a software toolchain for easy extraction of RDF data from existing information structures, such as classes or database records, and delivery of this data via web applications and services based on the popular framework Rails (Ruby et al., 2011). This tool chain is designed to be easy to integrate with existing libraries in a plugin-like fashion, in order to reduce the effort of integrating existing systems into Linked Data networks and infrastructures.

In Section 2 we describe the data collection, its provenance, its experimental setup and its levels of annotations. Then, Section 3 summarizes the steps from the internal representation of this (and other) multimodal data collections to a RDF representation served to the public web via HTTP. Some thoughts and prospects on how this system could be improved and distributed conclude the article.

## 2 The chat game experiment

### 2.1 About the chat game corpus

As a pilot test for the generation of RDF data in a large linguistic research project we selected a corpus resulting from a chat game experiment. This choice was motivated by several reasons:

1. The data set is compact and manageable, yet it contains data types and structures (e.g., multimodal and nonlinguistic interaction) that are still underrepresented in the Linked Data context.

2. It is heterogeneous, containing both language data and representations of actions and spatial entities.

3. The consent forms of the experiment contained clauses that permit a publication of the complete anonymized data sets. Without such explicit permissions, the publication even of anonymized derived data sets (such as transcriptions and annotations) is highly problematic especially in Germany. The chat game corpus is one of the few data sets with unproblematic consent forms. In addition, no video and audio recordings were created in this study, which regularly cause further problems considering anonymisation and protection of privacy for participants.

### 2.2 Participants and setup

28 adults (all native speakers of German) participated in pairs in the study (20 female, 8 male, mean age: 26). Data from several additional participants needed to be excluded due to various reasons. The players received course credit and/or a payment for their participation.

The chat game setup involves an object arrangement game paradigm with two players realised by a computer-mediated situation. Each participant sits at a computer terminal. The first participant (called the "chatter") has to describe target positions of objects on her screen with distinct colors and shapes to the second participant (the "slider") via chat messages. This second participant does not have access to the target configuration, resulting in the chatter's messages being the slider's only input. The slider is also not able to send messages. Their only mode of interaction is to move the game pieces onto the board, and into the correct positions.

The goal of the game is to reach the full target configuration of all objects by the technique described above. In each trial, eight rounds were played, with role switches between rounds.

### 2.3 Data structures

Primary data[1] essentially consists of an electronic log file of the activities performed by the participants. In particular, two types of actions were used: *chat messages* (including a time stamp and a string containing the message), and *movements of objects* (including a time stamp, an identifier of the object, and two pairs of coordinates, indicating the origin and the destination position on the board). The log file uses a custom XML format suited to the needs of the game (cf. Figure 2).

For each round, additional information about the respective target configuration was added to the log. A header contains further information about participants and a timestamp indicating the begin of the current trial.

Based on this automatically generated data, several annotations have been created:

[1]Terms like *primary* and *secondary data* are problematic when we go beyond classical face-to-face dialogues preserved in audio and video recordings. We use these terms in Lehmann's reading: "Primary linguistic data are [...] representations of [...] speech events with their spatio-temporal coordinates" (Lehmann, 2005, p. 187). However, his distinction between raw (=non-symbolic) and processed (=symbolic) data (Lehmann, 2005, pp. 205ff.) does not work for the data described here, because our raw data is in fact symbolic.

```
<match startTime="16.11.11 11:22">
  <round timeStarted="16.11.11 11:22" roundId="1">
    <chat time="+105" message="grauer kreis linke haelfte obere haelfte">
      <sentence value="fragment w/o verb" type="instruction" lok="spatial" id="s1">
        <parsetree id="parsetree1" tiefe="2" verzweigung="3.0" hoeflichkeit="2">
          <CNP>
            <NP>
              <ADJA lemma="grau">Grauer</ADJA>
              <NN lemma="Kreis">Kreis</NN>
            </NP>
            ...
          </CNP>
        </parsetree>
      </sentence>
    </chat>
    <move shape="gray_circle" from="-1,0" to="215,215" time="+133"/>
    <move shape="gray_circle" from="215,215" to="215,15" time="+136"/>
    ...
  </round>
  ...
</match>
```

Figure 2: A simplified example of the custom XML file format, containing one instruction and two subsequent moves (the second one being a correction).

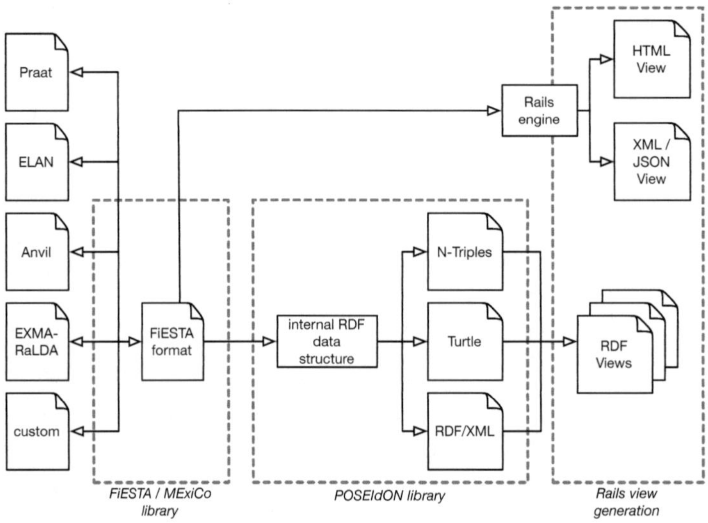


Figure 3: Architecture of the corpus management web application, grouped into scopes of responsibility of the respective libraries (FiESTA and POSEIdON).

1. A transformation of the written messages into orthographically and syntactically correct utterances. This was necessary for the parser (see below) to perform with an adequate accuracy.

2. Utterances were segmented into sentences and then parsed with the Stanford Parser (Klein and Manning, 2002; Klein and Manning, 2003), using the German version trained on the Negra corpus (Rafferty and Manning, 2008).

3. Syntactic and semantic properties of sentences were annotated, among them elaborateness (e.g., fragments and full sentences), speech acts (e.g., greetings, instructions, corrections, feedback) and localisation strategies – for instance, whether positions were described in relation to present objects ("to the right of the circle"), by describing absolute locations of the board itself ("into the bottom-left corner"), or by using metaphors (such as points of the compass, floors of buildings for rows: "south of the circle").

4. The parse trees were further annotated with basic tree measures (depth, breadth), and with an automatically generated quantitative measure of politeness, based on the occur-

rence of certain keywords, sentence types, and syntactic features.

Two annotators annotated the data. Some game instances were annotated by one of the annotators only, some by both of them. Differences were discussed with the experimenters, which lead to repeated correction and refinement of both annotations and annotation guidelines. This additional data was added to the XML files, as additional attributes or descendant elements to those already generated during experimentation.

Overall, the corpus contains 666 chat messages and 1,243 object moves. The parser created a total of 11,812 constituents (including terminal nodes) from the orthographically corrected chat messages (resulting in a total average of 17.75 constituent nodes per chat message).

## 3 From internal representations to RDF

### 3.1 Internal representation

We developed FiESTA (an acronym for "**f**ormat for **e**xtensive **s**patio**t**emporal **a**nnotations"), which takes into account various approaches, among them, the annotation graph approach (Bird and Liberman, 2001), the NITE object model (Evert et al., 2003), the speech transcription facilities of the TEI P5 specification (TEI Consortium, 2008), and the (X)CES standard (Ide et al., 2000). There were shortcomings in all these approaches that made it very difficult to express complex multimodal data structures. These shortcomings can also be found in theories and models that are more established in the Linked Data community, such as POWLA (Chiarcos, 2012) or LAF (Ide et al., 2003).

One of the most pressing problems is the restriction to a *single, flat stream or sequence of primary data* (called "text" in some approaches), or a *single, flat timeline*. In several data collections we need to support *multiple timelines*, especially in cases where multiple novel recording and tracking devices are used whose temporal synchronisation is nontrivial (because of irregular tracking intervals, computational delay, etc.). However, when working in a project with a limited duration, researchers are under time pressure, as a consequence, it can become necessary to perform analyses of data sets even before a working mechanism for complete, error-free synchronisation has been built by others. As an example, annotators might want to start the time-consuming transcription of speech as soon as possible, while others might make efforts to perform a categorization of automatically detected head gestures based on raw data generated by a novel tracker device. If it turns out that the time stamps in the tracker data are erroneous and cannot be aligned to the other ones using a simple linear transformation, there might be not enough time for their correction *before* annotators can start creating secondary data. Therefore, both groups need to start their work using their respective, isolated timelines if they do not want to put the project at risk. Simultaneously, the timeline of the tracking data must be aligned to that of the transcriptions in the background without modifying either of them.

The result are data sets that are based on different sets of time stamps, but belong to the same situation under investigation. A synchronisation of those different time stamps should be optional, and the original time stamps must be preserved as primary reference points at all times, even when a complete synchronisation can be achieved. With most of the given models, such an undertaking is either impossible, or it involves the alienation of model components (e.g., creation of phantom annotations being used as fake time points), which both inflates the resulting data structure and makes it less comprehensible. For instance, the annotation tool EXMARaLDA provides a mechanism for creating *time forks* (Schmidt and Wörner, 2005), but this is useful only for shorter stretches of simultaneous events surrounded by synchronised time points (e. g., for shorter segments of simultaneous speech), and not for timelines that might be completely independent from each other in the beginning and need to be merged and aligned later. Also, there are various potential reasons in a scientific workflow that call for the use of an annotation tool different from EXMARaLDA.

Also, in some cases there is need for the expression of spatial information parallel to temporal information. While this could be done by adding additional tiers with annotations, we consider it a cleaner and more logical solution to provide support for spatial (and other) axes on the same structural level as for timelines. This entails a modification of the present concept of the timeline towards a more general *scale* that also enables users to create spatial and abstract axes to which events and annotations can be aligned. There can be one or multiple scales, and each scale is given a unit, a dimension (e. g., time, or a spatial axis),

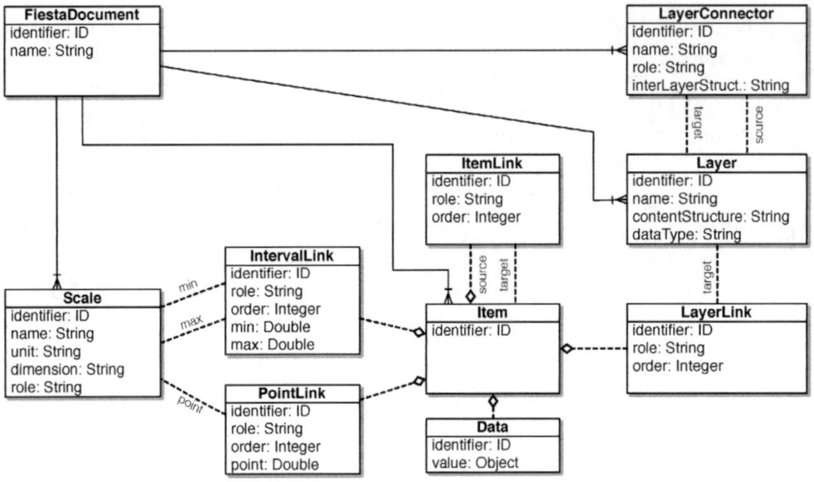


Figure 4: UML class diagram (simplified) of the FiESTA data model.

and a different level of measurement, following (Stevens, 1946). Scales can be left independent, or a synchronisation betweeen them can be expressed (e. g., a linear transformation between a video-frame-based scale and a millisecond-based one, or a manual alignment using explicit alignment points). A simplified version of the scale, and the other FiESTA classes and their relations is shown in the UML class diagram in Figure 4.

For the chat game data, three scales are used, one as a classic timeline, and two as a basis for coordinates on the two-dimensional game board. Chat messages, moves, and subsequent data sets are then imported as annotation items that are linked to points on these scales, and, in some cases, with a reference to other items.

### 3.2 A simple category registry

We established a simple web application serving as a minimalist concept registry. There, we collect and discuss concepts and categories for our data models as well as the multimodal phenomena that are (or are to be) modelled and described at our institution.[2]

The granularity of the modeling of these concepts (and also of properties) is roughly on the level of the components used in RDF Schema. A *category* consists of *(1)* an *identifier* (which automatically is suffixed to the ontology URI to create an URI for the category), *(2)* a human-readable *label*, *(3)* a human-readable *definition* (typically consisting of one or two sentences), *(4)* information about the *class hierarchy*, *(5)* information about possible *domains* and *ranges*, and *(6)* a number of *relations*, which express equivalence and similarity relations to other categories already existing outside the system (using appropriate vocabulary, such as `rdfs:seeAlso` or `owl:sameAs`).

We added some convenience methods for easy linking to some vocabularies or concept registries, among them, ISOcat (Windhouwer and Wright, 2012), XML Schema, Dublin Core, FOAF, and others.

At the moment, the ontology describing the FiESTA data model (cf. Subsection 3.1) contains 23 categories and 19 properties, resulting in 148 triples. The main part of which uses terms from the RDFS vocabulary for a description and definition of classes and properties. Links to appropriate ISOcat entries were created, as well as to the structuring components in the POWLA ontology. However, most of these links use a weak `rdfs:seeAlso` predicate rather than asserting a strict equivalence, mainly because of slightly deviating definitions, or because of different domain or range specifications.

At the moment, the main purpose of this concept registry is to provide an URL for each concept, and to serve a snippet of information when an HTTP request is sent to such an URL. Depending

[2]This registry is not meant to be a replacement for established solutions such as ISOcat, but rather as an antecedent tool for very early collection and discussion of concepts and terms within projects and groups. We believe that this tool, including additional mechanisms such as discussion boards, is a better place for early concept development. As soon as the first results emerge, categories can be transferred to systems such as ISOcat for presentation and discussion.

Figure 5: Screenshot of the simple category registry.

on the type of request, it delivers either a human-readable HTML document containing information about the concept (see Figure 5), or an RDF representation.

### 3.3 An RDF utility library

Within our systems, all transcription and annotation files are available in the pivotal representation format described above (see Section 3.1). They can be exported into all formats (a) for which an export routine is available and (b) that does not raise irresolvable format conversion errors. However, for the generation of RDF a different solution was chosen. We developed the POSEIdON library, containing modules that can be integrated into existing classes[3] in order to provide these classes and their instances with basic RDF information by using only a small set of configuring methods (see Figure 6 for an example of some POSEIdON directives and the resulting RDF). This can be useful if an existing library should be augmented with RDF information without modifying the existing source code.

For the representation of types and categories, the separate category registry described in 3.3 is used.

Typical use cases for POSEIdON directives are

- The definition of a URI for a class (used for type declarations of its instances).
- The definition of a URI scheme for instances of a class, based on a unique instance property.
- A mapping between instance variables and RDF snippets.
- Rules for a recursive RDF serialisation of member objects.

The low-level basis of POSEIdON is the established `rdf` library[4] which, in combination with various implementations of RDF writers, is used for collecting triples and exporting them to the respective variants of RDF documents. POSEIdON, by providing such a high-level interface, spares the user the creation and management of single RDF triples and graphs.

Several POSEIdON directives are added to the implementation of the FIESTA model. As a result, the RDF representation of a FiESTA document contains its complete contents represented as RDF triples (especially by using the recursive includes provided by POSEIdON).

There are already Ruby libraries that provide high-level support for RDF, such as the ActiveRDF library[5]. However, this library pursues a slightly different strategy by providing Ruby accessor methods to a data collection internally represented in RDF. In contrary, POSEIdON provides a simple way of getting an additional representation (in RDF) from an already existing library or data source in a *read-only* fashion, without modifying the source code of existing classes. Such data interfaces are typically based on XML documents or relational databases which are accessed with standard libraries (e.g., Nokogiri[6] for XML or ActiveRecord[7] for SQL databases). A modifi-

[3] We use Ruby's concept of *mixins*, which basically means the integration of source code contained in a module into an already existing class, without the need to alter the actual source code files of these classes.

[4] `https://github.com/ruby-rdf/rdf.`

[5] `http://activerdf.org/`

[6] `http://nokogiri.org.`

[7] `http://rubygems.org/gems/activerecord`

*(a)*

```
1  class Scale
2    include Poseidon
3    self_uri 'http://cats.acme.org/Scale'
4    rdf_property :identifier, 'http://cats.acme.org/identifier'
5    rdf_property :name, 'http://cats.acme.org/name'
6    rdf_property :unit, 'http://cats.acme.org/unit'
7    rdf_property :dimension, 'http://cats.acme.org/dimension'
8    rdf_property :mode, 'http://cats.acme.org/mode'
9    ...
10 end
```

*(b)*

```
@base <http://repo.acme.org/> .
@prefix cats: <http://cats.acme.org/> .
@prefix rdfs: <http://www.w3.org/2000/01/rdf-schema#> .

cats:Scale a rdfs:Class .

<resources/1#timeline> a cats:Scale;
  cats:identifier "timeline";
  cats:name "Timeline";
  cats:unit "s" ;
  cats:dimension "time";
  cats:mode "ratio".
```

Figure 6: Example of how POSEIdON works. *(a)* Usage of the POSEIdON library in a Ruby class to markup URIs (line 3) or to express rules for the export of instance properties (lines 4-8). — *(b)* The RDF resulting from these POSEIdON instructions. Some URLs are anonymized for review.

cation of such standard libraries just for an additional RDF representation would be out of proportion. POSEIdON's separate mixin strategy is a far cleaner approach.

### 3.4 Characteristics of the RDF representation

The resulting RDF representation (cf. the snippet in Figure 7) of the chat game corpus consists of approx. 300,000 triples (approx. 76,000 of these are data category annotations). A large number of those triples are necessary for the representation of the heavily interconnected phrase structure analyses of the chat messages. The category registry (cf. Subsection 3.2) is used for defining types of the entities contained in the corpus (as can be seen in the last lines of the code example in Figure 6b), where the predicates for the attributes come from the simple category registry described in Subsection 3.2.

### 3.5 Rails RDF integration

A web-based corpus management system is being developed in our project, which is based on Rails[8], a framework that uses the model-view-controller paradigm. In this system, RDF representations can easily be installed parallel to the standard HTML views and XML/JSON data representations by two rather simple steps:

1. Model classes need to be augmented with POSEIdON directives,

2. and additional routes and controller actions need to be defined for the paths and objects for which RDF should be delivered.

RDF data can be obtained by content negotiation either by adding a corresponding file suffix to the URI (if omitted HTML is returned by default), or by setting an appropriate `Accept` field in the HTTP request header. The actual generation of the RDF representation is done entirely by the strategy described in the previous section. The corresponding Rails controller then retrieves the RDF representation generated by POSEIdON, and generates a HTTP response (with the appropriate metadata, such as the content type).

For larger resources, Rails' built-in caching mechanisms can be used to further reduce the response time, in addition to the basic caching implemented in POSEIdON.

## 4 Conclusion

In this article, we present two main contributions: a chat game corpus that is not easily expressable in terms of classic corpus and annotation models that require a flat sequence of primary data elements (timeline items or tokens); and a toolchain that obtains RDF representations from data sets by attaching a modular interface to existing libraries

[8] `http://rubyonrails.org/`

```
<1> a cats:FiestaDocument;
  cats:hasItem <1#chat-5>,
    <1#round-1-move-7>,
    <1#round-1-move-8>;
  cats:hasLayer <1#chats>,
    <1#moves>,
    <1#sentences>,
    <1#parsedTrees>,
    <1#parsedPhrases>;
  cats:hasScale <1#timeline01>,
    <1#spatial_x>,
    <1#spatial_y>;
  cats:identifier "1" .

<1#timeline01> a cats:Scale;
  cats:identifier "timeline01";
  cats:name "Timeline";
  cats:unit "s" .

<1#moves> a cats:Layer;
  cats:identifier "moves";
  cats:name "Moves" .

<1#chat-5> a cats:Item;
  cats:hasData <1#chat-5-data>;
  cats:hasLayerLink <1#chat-5-layer>;
  cats:hasPointLink <1#chat-5-t>;
  cats:identifier "round-1-chat-5" .

<1#chat-5-data> a cats:Data;
  cats:stringValue "grauer kreis..." .

<1#chat-5-layer> a cats:LayerLink;
  cats:identifier "chat-5-layer";
  cats:target <1#chats> .

<1#chat-5-t> a cats:PointLink;
  cats:identifier "chat-5-t";
  cats:point 105,
  cats:target <1#timeline01> .
```

Figure 7: A snippet of the RDF representation generated by POSEIdON (corresponding to the chat message from Figure 2), with some context.

without modifying their actual source code. The principles of this toolchain have then been exemplified by taking the chat corpus data as a pilot data set. While our corpus and annotation data models have been under development for some years, the RDF publishing framework is still at an early stage. We believe that this data is a highly useful contributions to the linguistic and Linked Data community and that the resource is easier to use in a RDF form.

One of the more interesting aspects of the data is user-assigned data types, categories and structures used in singular annotation layers, especially when they go beyond the classic linguistic levels. While large vocabularies and ontologies for those have already been collected (for example, see the large number of syntactic and semantic concepts in ISOcat), there are hardly any entries for annotation schemes for gestures, eye movements, or other data coming from non-linguistic modalities. One of the main reasons is that morphosyntactic categories are far more established, and they are mainly agreed upon, at least to a degree sufficient for their integration into category registries. Research on non-linguistic modalities, on the other hand, is still at an early stage, and researchers have much more diverging sets of categories and definitions. As an example, the term *gesture* is used differently depending on the body limbs involved (especially, whether movements of the head and legs, knees, and feet should be subsumed unter this term, or whether there should be separate categories for them), so a premature nomenclature of categories based on only one of these definitions is not advisable.

Although the consequences of such novel research areas make it more difficult to create reliable concepts (and hence stable RDF), we are collaborating with researchers in these fields to collect first sets of categories for these modalities, which then are to be integrated into our category registry, and, when they are sufficiently agreed upon, also into the ISOcat system.

We believe that RDF-based representations especially of non-standard linguistic and multimodal resources (such as the chat game corpus, and other corpora, involving gestures, eye movements, and annotations of facial expressions) are a valuable gain for the Linguistic Linked Data community, even at such an early stage as described in this article.

## The data set

The simple category registry can be browsed at `http://cats.sfb673.org`. The pilot data set of the chat game in the draft format as described above will be made available at `http://phoibos.sfb673.org/corpora/ChatStudy`. However, the data set as well as the tools and libraries described above are under active development, so the data set is subject to change during the next months until a stable status of all related systems and tools is achieved.

## Acknowledgments

This research has been supported by the German Research Foundation (DFG) in the project X1 Multimodal Alignment Corpora: Statistical Modelling and Information Management of the Collaborative Research Centre (CRC) 673 Alignment in Communication at Bielefeld University, Germany.

## References

Steven Bird and Mark Liberman. 2001. A formal framework for linguistic annotation. *Speech communication*, 33(1-2):23–60.

Christian Chiarcos, Sebastian Hellmann, and Sebastian Nordhoff. 2011. Towards a Linguistic Linked Open Data cloud: The Open Linguistics Working Group. *TAL*, 52(3):245–275.

Christian Chiarcos. 2012. Powla: Modeling linguistic corpora in OWL/DL. In Elena Simperl, Philipp Cimiano, Axel Polleres, Oscar Corcho, and Valentina Presutti, editors, *The Semantic Web: Research and Applications*, volume 7295 of *Lecture Notes in Computer Science*, pages 225–239. Springer, Berlin/Heidelberg.

Stefan Evert, Jean Carletta, Timothy J. O'Donnell, Jonathan Kilgour, Andreas Vögele, and Holger Voormann. 2003. The NITE Object Model. In *Proceedings of the EACL Workshop on Language Technology and the Semantic Web*, pages 1–17.

Nancy Ide, Patrice Bonhomme, and Laurent Romary. 2000. XCES : An XML-based Encoding Standard for Linguistic Corpora. In *Proceedings of the Language Resources and Evaluation Conference (LREC)*, pages 825–830. ELRA.

Nancy Ide, Laurent Romary, and Eric de la Clergerie. 2003. International standard for a linguistic annotation framework. In *Proceedings of the HLT-NAACL 2003 workshop on Software engineering and architecture of language technology systems - Volume 8*, SEALTS '03, pages 25–30, Stroudsburg, PA, USA. Association for Computational Linguistics.

Dan Klein and Christopher D. Manning. 2002. Fast exact inference with a factored model for natural language parsing. *Advances in neural information processing systems*, 15:3—-10.

Dan Klein and Christopher D Manning. 2003. Accurate unlexicalized parsing. *Proceedings of the 41st Annual Meeting on Association for Computational Linguistics ACL 03*, 1(July):423–430.

Christian Lehmann. 2005. Data in linguistics. *The Linguistic Review*, 21(3-4):175–210.

Anna N. Rafferty and Christopher D. Manning. 2008. Parsing three German treebanks: Lexicalized and unlexicalized baselines. *Proceedings of the Workshop on Parsing German*, pages 40–46.

Sam Ruby, Dave Thomas, and David Heinemeier Hansson. 2011. *Agile Web Development with Rails 3.2*. Pragmatic Bookshelf, 4th edition.

Thomas Schmidt and K Wörner. 2005. Erstellen und Analysieren von Gespr{ä}chskorpora mit EXMARaLDA. *Gespr{ä}chsforschung*, 6:171–195.

S. S. Stevens. 1946. On the Theory of Scales of Measurement. *Science*, 103(2684):677–680.

TEI Consortium. 2008. *TEI P5: Guidelines for electronic text encoding and interchange*. TEI Consortium.

Menzo Windhouwer and Sue Ellen Wright. 2012. Linking to Linguistic Data Categories in ISOcat. In Christian Chiarcos, Sebastian Nordhoff, and Sebastian Hellmann, editors, *Linked Data in Linguistics*, pages 99–107. Springer Berlin Heidelberg.

# Linguistic Resources Enhanced with Geospatial Information

**Richard Littauer**
Computational Linguistics
University of Saarland
Saarbrücken, Germany
richard.littauer@gmail.com

**Boris Villazon-Terrazas***
Intelligent Software Components
iSOCO, S.A.
Av. del Partenon 16-18
Madrid, Spain
bvillazon@isoco.com

**Steven Moran**
Department of Linguistics
University of Zürich
Plattenstrasse 54, CH-8032
Zürich, Switzerland
steven.moran@uzh.ch

## Abstract

In this short report on language data and RDF tools, we describe the transformation process that we undertook to convert spreadsheet data about a group of endangered languages and where they are spoken in West Africa into an RDF triple store. We use RDF tools to organize and visualize these data on a world map, accessible through a web browser. The functionality we develop allows researchers to see where these languages are spoken and to query the language data. This type of development not only showcases the power of RDF, but it provides a powerful tool for linguists trying the solve the mysteries of the genealogical relatedness of the Dogon languages.

## 1 Introduction

Linked Data presents many opportunities to access and share data in different formats and for different purposes. In linguistics and related fields like cultural archaeology and population genetics, visualization of data points on maps is particularly beneficial in formulating hypotheses about data sets, particularly sparse ones, which is often the case in these fields. In this short report, we describe how we converted a spreadsheet that contains information about endangered Dogon languages and where they are spoken in small rural villages in Mali, West Africa, into an Resource Description Framework (RDF) triple store so that we could leverage other RDF tools to visualize these data. The result gives researchers a clearer picture of the dispersal of Dogon speakers and neighboring languages and we show that the spreadsheet-to-RDF conversion pipeline that we develop is applicable to any data set that can be combined with GPS coordinates.

*Ontology Engineering Group, Universidad Politécnica de Madrid, http://www.oeg-upm.net/

## 2 Background

In the visualization of language data, there has been work on displaying language differences on a broad scale, including presenting hierarchical and cross-linguistic data (7; 8), displaying related languages gathered from the World Atlas of Language Structures (WALS) by geographical proximity and relatedness (6), displaying word meanings on a map (9), and displaying the location of languages that contain some type of typological feature language locations on a world map (5). There has also recently been visualizations that display language relatedness and dialectology using lexical items and location together (11).

In this work we derive RDF from simple table data stored in a spreadsheet, leverage the ability of RDF graphs to be easily merged, and harness different RDF tools to display geospatial data in the map4rdf software, which is freely available and runs in the browser. In doing so, we provide detailed information about the location of villages in Mali in which Dogon languages are spoken. Dogon is an interesting language family because until recently there was very little that was known about these languages. In fact, until as late as 1989, Dogon appeared in reference books on African languages as if it were a single language (cf. (1; 2)). Current estimates from experts working in Mali is that there are now over 20 mutually unintelligble Dogon languages, with new varieties being "discovered" every year. However, the current genealogical relatedness of these languages is still unclear, as is the internal structure of the Dogon language family. Additionally, due to the typological characteristics of Dogon languages, such as these languages' lack of noun classes that are typical of sub-saharan West African languages in general or Dogon's SOV basic word order (instead of SVO like many of its neighbors), the position of the Dogon language family relative to other African language families remains unclear. Thus in disentangling the mysteries of how Dogon languages are related within their family, an interactive visual reference of where the languages are spoken is a useful tool for exploring avenues of possible genealogical decent due to geographic proximity and other effects like borrowing due to areal contact.

## 3 LLD Life Cycle

In this section we present the specification of the Linked Data Life Cycle presented in (10) as applied to linguistic resources to visualize them with geospatial information.

### 3.1 Linguistics Resources

Our data source consists of a spreadsheet containing GPS coordinates of villages where the different Dogon languages are spoken in Mali. It also contains information about each of these languages, such as the language name, ISO 639-3 language name identifier, the language family and family code, village name, etc. and it can be easily combined via ISO 639-3 codes with dictionary data from each language. These datasets come from the Dogon Languages Project and are freely available online.[1] They were collected by the Dogon Language Project team, mainly Jeffrey Heath, by on-ground reconnaissance or by using language maps; the provenance of each data point is noted in the spreadsheet.[2] Each set of data points per village is associated with a GPS coordinate and can thus be plotted on a world map. Because the set of Dogon languages that belong to the Dogon language family have been until recently poorly documented and described, information about where these languages are spoken in relation to each other can assist linguists in identifying the genealogical relatedness of these languages. The visualization of linguistic information on maps has been a successful method for generating and testing hypotheses (cf. (5)).

[1] `http://dogonlanguages.org`

[2] Steven Moran is affiliated with the Dogon Languages Project and he has worked with the geo spreadsheet data and with the LL-MAP project to bring these data online. See: `http://llmap.org/viewer.html?maps=472946.`

### 3.2 Specification

The process of publishing Linked Data has an iterative incremental life cycle model. Data sources must be identified and analyzed and entities in the data must be assigned a URI. A key element of Linked Data is also the ability to reuse and leverage data that has already been published as Linked Data. By identifying the schema of resources that are to be transformed into Linked Data, conceptual components and their relationships can be properly modeled into the RDF triple format. In the Dogon GPS spreadsheet, we were able to identify fields such as language name, ISO 639-3 code, language family and subfamily, alternative languages spoken in each village, village names, municipality, notes about the speaker's society, and geospatial information and assign them a URI. The spreadsheet also contains information about non-Dogon languages, which allows us to plot the current language contact situation between Dogon and surrounding languages. See Fig. 1.

All resources in the dataset are given dereferenceable URIs and we've attempted to use meaningful names instead of opaque ones. We also reuse URIs where we can, including using the General Ontology of Linguistic Description (GOLD) for morphosyntactic data descriptions (4).[3] The base URI structure uses the `http://linguistic.linkeddata.es/` namespace. Vocabulary elements are appended with `/ontology/{property|class}` and instances with `/dataset/resource/{r.type|r.name}`. We also reused URIs from the WGS84 Geo Basic Vocabulary for the representation of geospatial data.[4]

### 3.3 RDF Generation

Next, the spreadsheet data was transformed into RDF. First we imported the spreadsheet into MySQL. Then we defined a set of R2RML mappings. R2RML is a RDF-to-RDF mapping language and we used it to create mappings between elements in the MySQL database table from the spreadsheet and the RDF vocabulary that we defined.[5] Lastly, using the R2RML engine and morph,[6] we generated the RDF instances using the R2RML defined mappings. It is worth mentioning we are in the process of generating links with other

[3] `http://linguistics-ontology.org/.`

[4] `http://www.w3.org/2003/01/geo/`

[5] `http://www.w3.org/TR/r2rml/`

[6] `https://github.com/boricles/morph`

Figure 1: Data that contains villages in Mali with language information

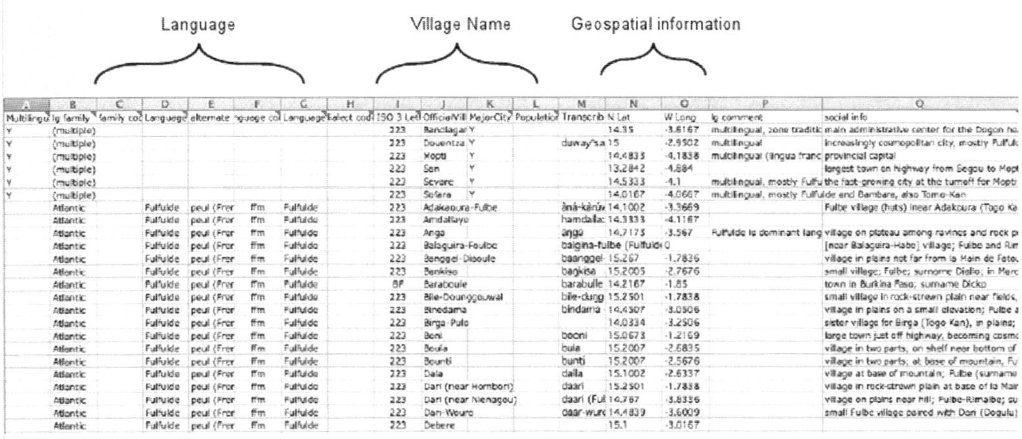


| A | B | C | D | E | F | G | H | I | J | K | L | M | N | O | P | Q |
|---|---|---|---|---|---|---|---|---|---|---|---|---|---|---|---|---|
| Multilingu | lg family | family coc | Language | alternate | nguage col | Language | dialect cod | ISO 3 Let | OfficialVill | MajorCity | Populatior | Transcrib | N Lat | W Long | lg comment | social info |
| Y | (multiple) | | | | | | | 223 | Bandiagar | Y | | | 14.35 | -3.6167 | multilingual, zone traditic | main administrative center for the Dogon ha |
| Y | (multiple) | | | | | | | 223 | Douentza | Y | | duway'sa | 15 | -2.9502 | multilingual | increasingly cosmopolitan city, mostly Fulfuk |
| Y | (multiple) | | | | | | | 223 | Mopti | Y | | | 14.4833 | -4.1838 | multilingual (lingua franc | provincial capital |
| Y | (multiple) | | | | | | | 223 | San | Y | | | 13.2842 | -4.884 | | largest town on highway from Segou to Mopt |
| Y | (multiple) | | | | | | | 223 | Sevare | Y | | | 14.5333 | -4.1 | multilingual, mostly Fulfu | the fast-growing city at the turnoff for Mopti |
| Y | (multiple) | | | | | | | 223 | Sofara | Y | | | 14.0167 | -4.0667 | multilingual, mostly Fulfulde and Bambara, also Tomo-Kan | |
| | Atlantic | | Fulfulde | peul (Frer | ffm | Fulfulde | | 223 | Adakoura-Fulbe | | | ànà-kànù | 14.1002 | -3.3669 | | Fulbe village (huts) near Adakoura (Togo Ka |
| | Atlantic | | Fulfulde | peul (Frer | ffm | Fulfulde | | 223 | Amdallaye | | | hamdalla: | 14.3333 | -4.1167 | | |
| | Atlantic | | Fulfulde | peul (Frer | ffm | Fulfulde | | 223 | Anga | | | aŋga | 14.7173 | -3.567 | Fulfulde is dominant lang | village on plateau among ravines and rock p |
| | Atlantic | | Fulfulde | peul (Frer | ffm | Fulfulde | | 223 | Balaguira-Foulbe | | | balgina-fulbe (Fulfuld | | 0 | | [near Balaguira-Habe] village; Fulbe and Rim |
| | Atlantic | | Fulfulde | peul (Frer | ffm | Fulfulde | | 223 | Benggel-Diboule | | | baanggel- | 15.267 | -1.7836 | | village in plains not far from la Main de Fatou |
| | Atlantic | | Fulfulde | peul (Frer | ffm | Fulfulde | | 223 | Benkiso | | | bagkise | 15.2005 | -2.7676 | | small village; Fulbe; surname Diallo; in Merc |
| | Atlantic | | Fulfulde | peul (Frer | ffm | Fulfulde | | BF | Baraboule | | | barabulle | 14.2167 | -1.85 | | town in Burkina Faso; surname Dicko |
| | Atlantic | | Fulfulde | peul (Frer | ffm | Fulfulde | | 223 | Bile-Dounggouwal | | | bile-dung | 15.2501 | -1.7838 | | small village in rock-strewn plain near fields, |
| | Atlantic | | Fulfulde | peul (Frer | ffm | Fulfulde | | 223 | Binedama | | | bindama | 14.4507 | -3.0506 | | village in plains on a small elevation; Fulbe a |
| | Atlantic | | Fulfulde | peul (Frer | ffm | Fulfulde | | 223 | Birga-Pulo | | | | 14.0334 | -3.2506 | | sister village for Birga (Togo Kan), in plains; |
| | Atlantic | | Fulfulde | peul (Frer | ffm | Fulfulde | | 223 | Boni | | | booni | 15.0673 | -1.2169 | | large town just off highway, becoming cosmo |
| | Atlantic | | Fulfulde | peul (Frer | ffm | Fulfulde | | 223 | Boula | | | bula | 15.2007 | -2.6835 | | village in two parts, on shelf near bottom of |
| | Atlantic | | Fulfulde | peul (Frer | ffm | Fulfulde | | 223 | Bounti | | | bunti | 15.2007 | -2.5676 | | village in two parts; at base of mountain, Fu |
| | Atlantic | | Fulfulde | peul (Frer | ffm | Fulfulde | | 223 | Dala | | | dalla | 15.1002 | -2.6337 | | village at base of mountain; Fulbe (surname |
| | Atlantic | | Fulfulde | peul (Frer | ffm | Fulfulde | | 223 | Dari (near Hombori) | | | daari | 15.2501 | -1.7838 | | village in rock-strewn plain at base of la Mair |
| | Atlantic | | Fulfulde | peul (Frer | ffm | Fulfulde | | 223 | Dari (near Nienagou) | | | daari (Ful | 14.767 | -3.8336 | | village on plains near hill; Fulbe-Rimaibe; su |
| | Atlantic | | Fulfulde | peul (Frer | ffm | Fulfulde | | 223 | Dari-Wouro | | | daar-wurc | 14.4839 | -3.6009 | | small Fulbe village paired with Dari (Dogulu) |
| | Atlantic | | Fulfulde | peul (Frer | ffm | Fulfulde | | 223 | Debere | | | | 15.1 | -3.0167 | | |

datasets, such as WALS and DBpedia.

### 3.4 Publication

The RDF data that we generated is stored in a triple store with the Virtuoso software, which we use to publish the data online.[7] Integrated with Pubby,[8] Virtuoso allows us to leverage content management to serve up machine-readable and human consumable webpages that contain information about each village, such as which languages are spoken there, where the village is located, additional information about the society, etc.[9] Virtuoso also provides a SPARQL endpoint[10] with which we can query and share the data.

### 3.5 Exploitation

Following the previous steps of specification, RDF generation and publication, we expose the RDF data, enhanced with GPS coordinates, using map4rdf.[11] map4rdf is a maps viewer of RDF resources with geometrical information built on OpenStreetMap[12] and it can be used to visualize information in RDF datasets. Additionally, it is extensible with Google app plugins. The parameters of map4rdf must be set so that the application knows where to locate the endpoint of Dogon data in RDF (that we set up with Virutoso) and which geometry model that we are using (since there different standards for geo-mapping). With the parameters set, a user can open the map4rdf application in his or her web browser and explore the location of villages where Dogon are spoken.[13] Fig. 2 provides an illustration.

Each point on the map comes from GPS coordinates in the original spreadsheet, which have been transformed into RDF triples and stored in a triple store with Virtuoso. This triple store can be queried with SPARQL or its endpoint can be given as an endpoint for programs like map4rdf to access its data contents. Each pin in Fig. 2 can be clicked on, showing the village name, its latitude and longitude, and a link for more information about the language. This is shown in Fig. 3.

When clicking on the link for more information, a request is sent to the SPARQL endpoint for all information in the RDF triple store about that particular village. When accessing the data through map4rdf, the endpoint knows through content management to return an HTML page that displays the query results, as shown in Fig. 4.

## 4 Summary

We have briefly shown here a workflow to transform data from a simple spreadsheet into an RDF triple store that can queried using a SPARQL endpoint, and an application called map4rdf that uses this endpoint with GPS coordinates to visualize RDF data on a world map. Moreover, the tools

[7] http://virtuoso.openlinksw.com/

[8] http://www4.wiwiss.fu-berlin.de/pubby/

[9] See for example the page on the village Boni: hhttp://linguistic.linkeddata.es/mlode/resource/Village/Boni

[10] http://linguistic.linkeddata.es/sparql

[11] https://github.com/boricles/linked-data-visualization-tools

[12] http://www.openstreetmap.org/

[13] The map4rdf instantiation for the Dogon villages resides at: http://geo.linkeddata.es/map4rdf-dogon/.

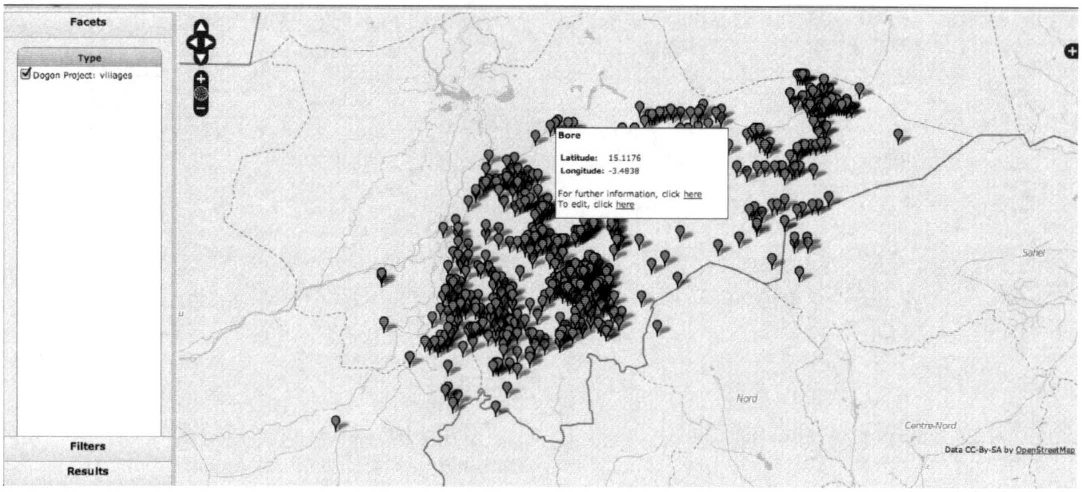


Figure 2: Visualization of the Dogon villages

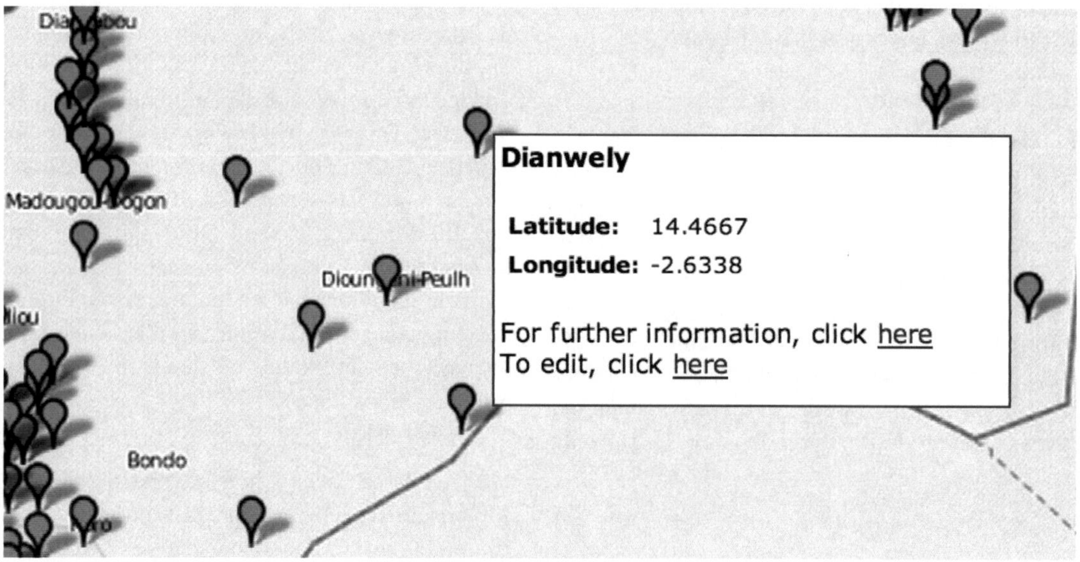


Figure 3: Clicking on a pin

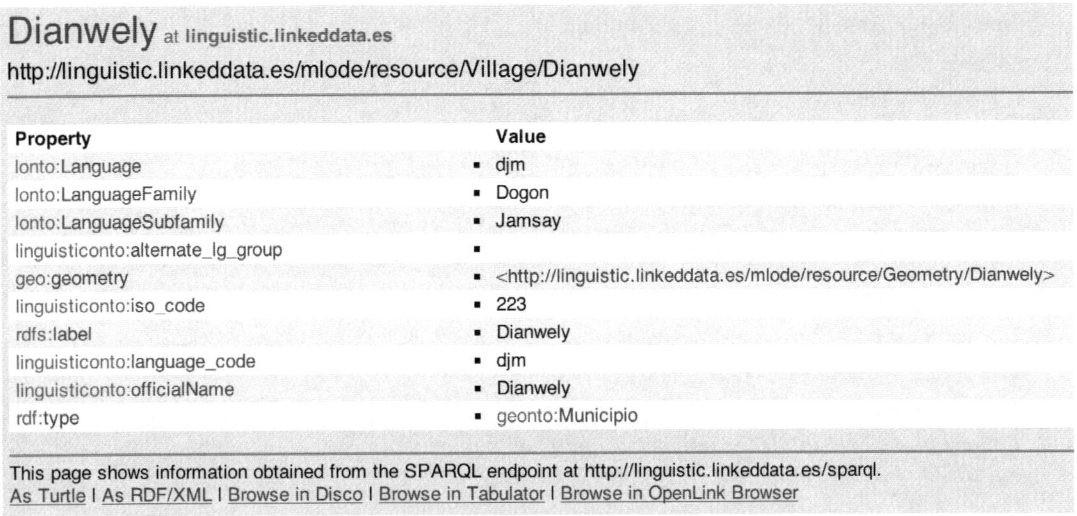


Figure 4: More information about a village

that we have used here are open source and freely available. Converting linguistic data into RDF can be a straightforward process and we have shown the steps and some tools to assist in that transformation. There is much data available about languages and their typological features on the Web, which are often available in simple .csv formats. For example, the contents of World Atlas of Language Structures (WALS)[14] (5) have been converted from .csv to RDF and are available through the MLODE SPARQL endpoint.[15] It was a trivial task for us to set up map4rdf to point at the WALS RDF data, so that we could also visualize its contents, which contain over 2000 languages' data points. Whereas the online version of WALS already contains maps of typological features of languages, their use is limited and by leveraging RDF as we have with WALS and the Dogon data, we can easily combine these disparate datasets, so that, for example, we can merge data about languages and their typological features from both datasets. This allows us to visualize not only the villages where Dogon languages are spoken, but linguistic features of languages spoken in this area of Mali encoded in WALS. This mashup provides even more detailed information about the features of these different languages, which provides another important data source in untangling the mystery of why Dogon languages are so different than other language families in West Africa. It also shows the power of encoding data in RDF and leveraging RDF tools.

[14]`http://wals.info`

[15]`http://mlode-sparql.nlp2rdf.org/sparql`

## References

[1] J. Bendor-Samuel, E. J. Olsen, and A. R. White. Dogon. In J. Bendor-Samuel, editor, *The Niger-Congo Languages–A Classification and Description of Africa's Largest Language Family*, pages 169–177. University Press of America, Lanham, Maryland, 1989.

[2] R. Blench. A survey of Dogon languages in Mali: overview. *OGMIOS*, 26:14–15, 2005.

[3] A. de León, F. Wisniewki, B. Villazón-Terrazas, and O. Corcho. Map4rdf - Faceted Browser for Geospatial Datasets. In *Proceedings of the First Workshop on USING OPEN DATA*. W3C, June 2012.

[4] S. Farrar and D. T. Langendoen. A Linguistic Ontology for the Semantic Web. *GLOT International*, 7:97–100, 2003.

[5] M. Haspelmath, M. Dryer, D. Gil, and B. Comrie, editors. *The World Atlas of Language Structures Online*. Max Planck Digital Library, Munich, 2008.

[6] R. Littauer, R. Turnbull, and A. Palmer. Visualising typological relationships: Plotting wals with heat maps. In *Proceedings of the EACL 2012 Workshop on the Visualization of Linguistic Patterns*, page 4, Avignon, France,

April 2012. Association for Computational Linguistics.

[7] C. Rohrdantz, M. Hund, T. Mayer, B. Wälchli, and D. A. Keim. The world's languages explorer: Visual analysis of language features in genealogical and areal contexts. *Comp. Graph. Forum*, 31(3pt1):935–944, June 2012.

[8] C. Rohrdantz, T. Mayer, M. Butt, F. Plank, and D. A. Keim. Comparative visual analysis of cross-linguistic featuretures. In J. Kohlhammer and D. A. Keim, editors, *Proceedings of the International Symposium on Visual Analytics Science and Technology (EuroVAST 2010). The DEFINITIVE VERSION is available at diglib.eg.org.*, pages 27–32, 2010.

[9] R. Therón, L. Fontanillo, A. Esteban, and C. Segun. Visual analytics: A novel approach in corpus linguistics and the nuevo diccionario histórico del español. In *III Congreso Internacional de Lingstica de Corpusi*, 2011.

[10] B. Villazón-Terrazas, L. Vilches-Blázquez, O. Corcho, and A. Gómez-Pérez. Methodological Guidelines for Publishing Government Linked Data Linking Government Data. In D. Wood, editor, *Linking Government Data*, chapter 2, pages 27–49. Springer New York, New York, NY, 2011.

[11] M. Wieling, J. Nerbonne, and R. H. Baayen. Quantitative social dialectology: Explaining linguistic variation geographically and socially. *PLoS ONE*, 6(9):e23613, 09 2011.

# Faust.rdf - Taking RDF literally

**Timm Heuss**
University of Plymouth,
Plymouth, United Kingdom
`Timm.Heuss@{plymouth.ac.uk, web.de}`

## Abstract

This paper undertakes the modelling experiment of translating excerpts of the natural language play - "Faust" by Johann Wolfgang von Goethe - into a RDF structure, so that it is accessible by machines on a word or concept level. Thereby, it is crucial that statements made in the logic of the play can be distinguished from the usual, general purpose Linked Open Data. The goal is to find a standard compliant solution, stressing RDF's central role in the Web of Data as a format for arbitrary data.

## 1 Introduction

The Resource Description Framework (RDF) is meant to be the ideal data format for arbitrary information in the Web of Data, since it is open, machine-readable, non-proprietary and a World Wide Web Consortium (W3C) standard. In Berners-Lees popular five star ranking system, rankings above three stars can only be archived if the data is published in RDF (Berners-Lee, 2009).

Thus, this format plays an important role in many data portals[1], which publish data according to the Linked Open Data (LOD) paradigm.

RDF is the approved and commonly known method of making information of any kind available to machines, so they can access it in a structured way.

## 2 Motivation

However, when talking about publishing natural language content as LOD, the simple but very strict design goal of structuring information for machines is often violated. Whenever the natural language itself is not the modelling subject, datasets usually treat RDF as a meta data format, where accompanying natural language content remains either semi-structured (like in the Bible Ontology[2]) or entirely unstructured (like in Gutenberg in RDF[3]), in fields of the type `xs:string`. In both cases, natural language content is still not readable (in terms of accessible in a structured way) by machines - despite the fact that RDF is used. It's just displayable, just like it is displayable in the "eyeball Web" (Breslin et al., 2009, p. 82).

## 3 Idea

This paper is about the experiment Faust.rdf. Thereby, the author tries to strictly apply the central design principle of the RDF format, namely structuring information in a machine readable way, to natural language content, that would otherwise just be stored as `xs:string`. This means that natural language needs to be converted in a very structured variant, that formalizes the content on word or concept level. To choose a realistic scenario, the source material that is being formalized is the play "Faust: The First Part of the Tragedy" (Faust I) from Johann Wolfgang von Goethe[4].

The idea and the selected kind of source text is heavily inspired by the work of Richard Light, who expressed the works of Shakespeare as LOD (Light, 2013). In contrast to this paper, there is one important difference: The resulting LOD of Light semi-structures Shakespeare's texts, having selected an actual text line as smallest modelling atomicity. When taking RDF's principles literally, this goes, in the opinion of the author, not far enough.

[1] Popular Open Data portals are `http://data.gov.uk/` (accessed 2013-07-05), `http://data.gov.uk/` (accessed 2013-07-05) or `https://www.govdata.de/` (accessed 2013-07-05).

[2] `http://datahub.io/dataset/bible-ontology` (accessed 2013-07-05).

[3] `http://wifo5-04.informatik.uni-mannheim.de/gutendata/directory/texts` (accessed 2013-07-05).

[4] `http://en.wikipedia.org/wiki/Faust:_The_First_Part_of_the_Tragedy` (accessed 2013-07-06).

Faust.rdf is about trying to model selected statements of Faust with RDF's capacities, with the atomicity of words or concepts. The goal of identifying the status quo of RDF for this kind of modelling subjects and documenting experienced challenges. Resulting RDF statements would, of course, not replace or constitute the entire source text. Instead, it would form a novel kind of secondary source in the spirit of the Open Data movement. This is comparable to Wikipedia, where there are articles in English and, alternatively, in Simple English[5].

## 4 Requirements

The figures 1a and 1b show the definition the two central entities, that are considered in the following formalization of a literature work:

$$verse(time, source, speaker, type, act) \quad (1a)$$

$$content[verse](statements) \quad (1b)$$

The basic unit of a text is a *verse*, that refers to a certain *time* measure (which is, in poetry, usually the verse number). It's also constituted by the *source*, the human readable original text, an optional definition of the *speaker*, the *type* of the verse (whether it is a question, a proposition or a scene description) and the *act* in which the verse is subordinated to.

This structure is very generic and is comparable to other, semi-structured approaches, like Light's Shakespeare experiment (2013). In contrast to those approaches, the entity *content* is defined, consisting of actual *statements* about the natural language content of a play and the referenced *verse*, as defined above.

The goal is to produce five-star LOD (Berners-Lee, 2009) that represents the entities in the script of the play as close as possible. Thereby, links to external references are important and the underlying poetry needs to be understood properly. This is in contrast to automatic RDF extraction approaches like FRED[6] or the controlled vocabularies Attempto Controlled English[7] and Processible English[8], that try to extract and to represent logical relations out of a given natural language text.

[5] http://simple.wikipedia.org/wiki/Main_Page (accessed 2013-07-06).

[6] http://wit.istc.cnr.it/stlab-tools/fred/ (accessed 2013-07-07).

[7] http://attempto.ifi.uzh.ch/site/description/ (accessed 2013-07-07).

[8] http://web.science.mq.edu.au/~rolfs/peng/ (accessed 2013-07-07).

As this is a novel endeavor, the translation of Faust into RDF statements is a manual process.

## 5 Design

The solution consists of two design decisions: The exact way of how the two defined entities verse (1a) and content (1b) are converted into a RDF structure, and which LOD datasets are employed in that process.

### 5.1 RDF structure

In this modelling approach, context is very important. A verse in poetry does not contain general-purpose world knowledge, but very play- and actor-specific, subjective views on a fictional world - that could even turn out to be wrong at a later point.

To respect this fact in the realm of RDF, N-Quads (Cyganiak et al., 2008) can be used. N-Quads extend the *subject*, *predicate* and *object* of RDF triples with the fourth component *context*, which allows an optional definition of context for those triples.

RDF triples about the verse are within the context of the entire play (1a), and it is sufficient to rely on the basic building blocks of the Semantic Web (Allemang and Hendler, 2011, p. 9) by choosing an adequately unique Uniform Resource Identifier (URI). Instead, statements about the actual content (1b) of a certain verse are where protagonists claim, ask or lie. Thus it is a good idea of having a special handling for this kind of statements, i.e. putting the RDF triples about the content in a quadruple, in the context of a certain verse.

### 5.2 LOD datasets

LOD portals, in this case Datahub[9], make it very easy nowadays to find the linguistically grounded and interlinked data sets for the given use case.

In this project, entities are linked with lemonUby[10], one of the most comprehensive resources, especially in linking verbs. In addition, DBpedia[11] has an entry for entire play[12], which is used as namespace for all Faust.rdf statements.

[9] http://datahub.io/ (accessed 2013-07-07).

[10] http://lemon-model.net/lexica/uby/ (accessed 2013-08-30).

[11] http://dbpedia.org/About (accessed 2013-07-07).

[12] http://dbpedia.org/page/Faust:_The_First_Part_of_the_Tragedy (accessed 2013-07-07).

Besides these LOD datasets, the source texts in natural language are taken from eBooks@Adelaide[13] (English) and Wikisource[14] (German).

## 6 Implementation

In this section, the findings of the preceding sections are tested with an exemplary RDF translation in the N-Quads notation. Thereby, the verses 1323 to 1325 of Faust are excerpted. In the English source text, they read (Goethe, 2005):

```
      FAUST
1323   This was the poodle's real core,
1324   A travelling scholar, then?
       The casus is diverting.
      MEPHISTOPHELES
1325   The learned gentleman I bow
       before
```

In the following, the RDF translation of worthwhile parts is documented. Please note that triples are abbreviated using prefixes[15], even though the N-Quads notation format does not allow them. The full translation of verses 1323 to 1325 is available at GitHub[16].

### 6.1 Common statements

First, the protagonists Faust and Mephistopheles are introduced as instances of person respectively devil:

```
<:Faust> <rdf:type>
  <ubywn:WN_LexicalEntry_15513> .

<:Mephistopheles> <rdf:type>
  <ubywn:WN_LexicalEntry_134036> .
```

### 6.2 Verse Metadata

Translation of the verses follow a given, straightforward pattern, as introduced 1a on the preceding page. First, the source text is defined as human readable label:

```
<:verse1323> <rdfs:label>
  "This was the poodle's real core"@en .
```

Line number and act are defined in a similar way and are omitted in this paper. However, translating the certain kind for verse 1324 is especially notable, as this verse contains a question as well as an assertion. After defining verse 1324 in the fashion of verse 1323 above, there are two variations:

```
<:verse1324a> <rdfs:subClassOf>
  <:verse1324> .
<:verse1324b> <rdfs:subClassOf>
  <:verse1324> .
# "verse1324a is a question"
<:verse1324a> <rdf:type>
  <ubywn:WN_LexicalEntry_153777> .
# "verse1324b is a statement"
<:verse1324b> <rdf:type>
  <ubywn:WN_LexicalEntry_81754> .
```

The per-verse meta data is completed by the assignment of the according speakers, e.g.:

```
# "Faust asks verse1324a"
<:Faust> <ubyvn:VN_LexicalEntry_1993>
  <:verse1324a> .
```

### 6.3 Verse content

As mentioned, the verse content is defined with N-Quads, having the individual verses as respective context. This allows to distinguish between general purpose world knowledge, like the fact that the play Faust has a certain verse 1324, from elements of the play, like the fact that the devil is a poodle. This way, it is also possible to encode a lie: Just like in the previous section, a certain verse would not be defined as a statement, but as a lie. Thanks to the context notation, further RDF statements can be made within the context of this verse, respectively in the context of this lie.

The following statements reflect the content of the verses 1323 to 1325:

**"This was the poodle's real core"**

```
# "Poodle is a disguise"
<:Poodle> <rdf:type>
 <ubywn:WN_LexicalEntry_48830>
  <:verse1323> .
# "Poodle transforms into Mephistopheles
<:Poodle> <ubywn:WN_LexicalEntry_90692>
    <:Mephistopheles> <:verse1323> .
```

**"A travelling scholar, then?
The casus is diverting."**

```
# "Mephistopheles is a travelingScholar"
<:Mephistopheles> <rdf:type>
  _:travelingScholar <:verse1324a> .
# "travelingScholar is a scholar"
_:travelingScholar <rdf:type>
  <ubyvn:WN_LexicalEntry_99198> .
# "travelingScholar is a traveler"
_:travelingScholar <rdf:type>
  <ubywn:WN_LexicalEntry_115017> .

# "Verse 1324a amuses Faust"
<:verse1324a>
```

[13] http://ebooks.adelaide.edu.au/ (accessed 2013-08-30).

[14] http://de.wikisource.org/wiki/Faust_I (accessed 2013-07-07).

[15] Besides the common rdf and rdfs prefixes, the following are used: ubywn = http://lemon-model.net/lexica/uby/wn/, ubyvn= http://lemon-model.net/lexica/uby/vn/. Default namespace is http://dbpedia.org/page/Faust_I

[16] https://github.com/heussd/faust.rdf/blob/master/src/main/resources/faust.nq (accessed 2013-08-19).

```
  <ubyvn:VN_LexicalEntry_2516>
    <:Faust>  <:verse1324b> .
```

**"The learned gentleman I bow before"**

```
# "Verse 1324a is true"
<:verse1324a> <rdf:type>
  <ubywn:WN_LexicalEntry_53631>
    <:verse1325> .

# "Mephistopheles appreciates Faust"
<:Mephistopheles>
  <ubyvn:VN_LexicalEntry_731>
    <:Faust> <:verse1325> .
```

## 7 A critical view

This is a very first step and the translation might be neither perfect nor complete. While modelling the verse metadata is a not very exciting task, the crucial thing is to have a working context pattern for the actual content RDF statements.

It can be stated that RDF is, together with the N-Quads notation, indeed able to represent a fictional play, including the conditional statements that it involves. It is notable that N-Quads can considered to be a shortcut for a number of reification statements, as stated by an early mailing list posting (Palmer, 2001). Therefore, even pure RDF could able to cope with contexts, even though the resulting code would be much more complicated.

In the previous attempt[17], YAGO2[18] in combination of DBpedias subproject Wiktionary[19] was used to interlink entities. However, because both datasets still certain words, some translation results didn't reflect the play properly.

Not being able to use prefix-namespaces, however, bloated up results unnecessarily and affected human readability. Having available assisting editor tools during the manual translation would have made things easier or at least faster. There is a clear lack of assistive, cross-disciplinary Natural Language Processing (NLP) and LOD tools, that are both user friendly and still can cope with giant, distributed datasets like YAGO2 and DBpedia.

## 8 Conclusion

When storing natural language, RDF still today plays a metadata role: Texts remain un- or semi-structured, stored in `xs:string`-fields, inaccessible to machines just like before the "eyeball Web".

This paper undertakes the experiment of translating a natural language script of play, excerpts of Faust by Johann Wolfgang von Goethe, on a word or concept level into a RDF structure, so that it is accessible by machines, in the spirit of five-star LOD. Thereby, it is crucial that fictional statements made by protagonists of the play can be distinguished from the other, general-purpose statements containing world knowledge.

With N-Quads, in association with a number of datasets like lemonUby and DBpedia, a convenient solution is successfully designed and exemplary tested. This demonstrates the maturity of the used datasets as well as the RDF format, confirming it as a credible backbone of the LOD movement. Nevertheless, some issues are identified, regarding interdisciplinary tool support for the NLP and LOD domain.

## 9 Outlook

Having available large amounts of natural language texts, structured like proposed in this paper, would have a number of benefits.

As mentioned, in the role of a secondary source, RDF statements could give users hints in understanding the idea of the original text. This is especially important for very old texts, that use old-fashioned variants of natural languages that, eventually, only historians can understand.

Another benefit is that it could enable even non-experts to answer in-depth questions on the text, e.g. in case of Faust I: "In which scene does the devil appear the first time?"[20]

Also, knowledge-based NLP applications could become more common, like a Machine Translation approach, for example, which relies on the ability to extract human readable stories from RDF (Harriehausen-Mühlbauer and Heuss, 2012).

## 10 Acknowledgements

The author wants to thank Richard Light, Bernhard G. Humm and Kerstin Reinking for the inspiring discussions. He also thanks the LDL2013 reviewers for the very useful suggestions, which significantly improved this work.

[17] See GitHub diff page at https://github.com/heussd/faust.rdf/commit/93f06b43c4212f0835171ab17ca89f22719aa2e4 (accessed 2013-08-30).

[18] http://www.mpi-inf.mpg.de/yago-naga/yago/ (accessed 2013-07-07).

[19] http://dbpedia.org/Wiktionary (accessed 2013-07-07).

[20] In Faust I, answering the question of the first appearance of the devil requires a deeper text understanding, as he first appears in form of a dog, that later transforms into the devil.

## References


[Allemang and Hendler2011] Dean Allemang and James A. Hendler. 2011. *Semantic Web for the Working Ontologist - Effective Modeling in RDFS and OWL, Second Edition*. Morgan Kaufmann.

[Berners-Lee2009] Tim Berners-Lee. 2009. Linked Data. Webpage, June.

[Breslin et al.2009] John G. Breslin, Alexandre Passant, and Stefan Decker. 2009. *The Social Semantic Web*. Springer, Berlin.

[Cyganiak et al.2008] Richard Cyganiak, Andreas Harth, and Aidan Hogan. 2008. N-Quads: Extending N-Triples with Context, July.

[Goethe2005] Johann Wolfgang Von Goethe. 2005. *Faust*. The Project Gutenberg.

[Harriehausen-Mühlbauer and Heuss2012] Bettina Harriehausen-Mühlbauer and Timm Heuss. 2012. Semantic Web based Machine Translation. In *Proceedings of the Joint Workshop on Exploiting Synergies between Information Retrieval and Machine Translation (ESIRMT) and Hybrid Approaches to Machine Translation (HyTra)*, pages 1–9, Avignon, France, April. Association for Computational Linguistics.

[Light2013] Richard Light. 2013. Open Data on the Web position paper. In *W3C Workshop on the Open Data on the Web, 23 - 24 April 2013, Google Campus, Shoreditch, London, United Kingdom*.

[Palmer2001] Sean B. Palmer. 2001. Nquads. mailinglist, 08.

# RDFization of Japanese Electronic Dictionaries and LOD

**Seiji Koide**
Research Organization of Information and Systems
2-1-2 Hitotsubashi, Chiyoda-ku, Tokyo
koide@nii.ac.jp

**Hideaki Takeda**
National Institute of Informatics
2-1-2 Hitotsubashi, Chiyoda-ku, Tokyo
takeda@nii.ac.jp

## Abstract

This paper describes the practice and the reality of OWL conversion of Japanese WordNet and Japanese dictionary IPAdic. The outcomes of OWL conversion are linked to DBpedia Japanese dataset using lexical word matching. The difficulty originating from the specialty of Japanese, which is shareable by non-English languages, is focused. The potential of LOD in linguistics is also discussed. The goal of our study on Linguistics by LOD is to provide an open and rich environment in linguistics that propels multi-lingual studies for linguistics researchers and bottom-up style ontology buildings for ontologists.

## 1 Introduction

The traditional study of linguistics in Japanese is somehow domestic and not open so far to unrelated people. Linguistics by Linked Open Data (LLOD) has a potential to break this tradition and to open linguistic resources to broad researchers unlimited within linguistics. However, Japanese linguistic LOD embraces special difficulties that arise from specialties of the nature of Japanese. These difficulties are not only limited to Japanese but also common to non-English languages.

In this paper, we describe the practice and the reality of OWL conversion of Japanese WordNet and Japanese dictionary IPAdic. To make the outcomes into LOD, we linked the entities of them to DBpedia Japanese and made them accessible on WWWs.

In the next section, we summarize what is LOD and address the benefit of LLOD along with the introduction of DBpedia Japanese. Our work of RDFization of Japanese WordNet and linkage to DBpedia Japanese are described in Section 3. Section 4 introduces the RDFization of IPAdic and the linkage to DBpedia Japanese. Section 5 presents the publication of our work as LOD. Related work is discussed in Section 6, and Section 7 finally gives the summary and the discussion for future work.

## 2 LOD and DBpedia

### 2.1 Linguistic LOD and Five Stars

In Linked Open Data (LOD), Tim Berners-Lee, the inventor of the Web and Linked Data initiator, suggested a five-star deployment scheme.[1] In this view, there was no LOD resource for Japanese linguistics up to this study. EDR (Yokoi, 1995) by Japan Electronic Dictionary Research Center and lately NICT, GoiTaikei (Ikehara, et al., 1997) by NTT, and a Japanese corpora by National Institute for Japanese Language and Linguistics[2] are provided in machine readable forms but not in free use. However, the property of Japanese WordNet (Isahara, et al., 2008), IPAdic/NAIST-jdic (Matsumoto, et al., 1999), and UniDic (Den, et al., 2008) is in free use.

Based on the five-star scheme for LOD, we can deduce the condition of making LOD of a domain as follows.

1. Are materials in the domain open (free in use)?
2. Is the structure of materials disclosed being sufficient for RDFization?
3. Is it possible to name the components by controllable URIs?
4. Is it possible to make linkage to other resources?

Therefore, Japanese WordNet, IPAdic/NAIST-jdic, and UniDic deserve the conversion to

[1] See http://5stardata.info/.

[2] See, http://www.ninjal.ac.jp/corpus_center/kotonoha.html.

RDF/OWL data format in order to let them turn data resources in LOD, namely making URIs of all components in dictionaries with controllable domain names and letting them enable to be referenced on the webs (i.e., *dereferenceable*). Whereby, we can enjoy Japanese linguistic resources in the new paradigm of LOD.

We propose the benefit of LLOD as follows.

- Enables the sharing of linguistic resources.
- Enables the comparison of linguistic resources among them over silos of different dictionaries in their own definitions.
- Enables the usage of linguistic resources with other non-linguistic resources (e.g., DBpedia).
- Enables the development of ontologies starting at the lexical level for multiple vocabulary sets.

### 2.2 DBpedia Japanese as LOD Hub

DBpedia Japanese is a database generated from Japanese Wikipedia using DBpedia Information Extraction Framework (DIEF).[3] Although there was significant delay in the deployment of DBpedia Japanese, it was launched in 2012 by our colleagues at National Institute of Informatics (NII). Since then, all LOD resources in Japan are being linked to the DBpedia Japanese and it has become the hub of LOD-cloud in Japan as English DBpedia (Bizer, et al., 2009) is in the world. In Japan, there are currently 23 data sets linked directly or indirectly to DBpedia Japanese, which contains 77,445,359 triples, at the time of writing this paper.

## 3 RDFization of Japanese WordNet and Links to DBpedia Japanese

### 3.1 Practice of RDFization

In addition to RDF syntax[4] and RDF semantics[5], we have discovered some pragmatics on RDFization in LOD. General ones over diverse domains are described in Heath and Bizer (2011). In this section, we describe more specific practices in RDFization of Japanese resources.

#### 3.1.1 Normalization of UNICODE

As known by the popular picture of Semantic Web Layer Cake[6], UNICODE is the proper character encoding set of Semantic Web and LOD. However, it is not known that strings in an RDF graph should be in Normal Form C (NFC) of UNICODE.[7] Otherwise, serious problems may happen in Japanese and other non-English languages. For example, 'ö' that is located in Basic Plane 0 is encoded to U+00F6 but it is also printed by octets U+006F (Latin small letter o) + U+0308 (combining dieresis). Then, we may miss string matching "Gödel" between one that consists of U+00F6 and the other that consists of U+006F + U+0308. The same thing can happen in case of Plato (Πλάτων) in which 'ά' may be U+03AC, or the combination of U+03B1(Greek small letter alpha) and U+0301(combining acute accent). In Japanese, 'が'(U+304C) may be represented by { か + ゛ }, and 'ぷ'(U+3077) may be represented by { ふ + ゜ }. The normalization of NFC solves this ambiguity of character strings in UNICODE.

#### 3.1.2 Supplementary Ideographic Plane in UNICODE

Several extended *kanji* characters are located in Supplementary Ideographic Plane of UNICODE, which is implemented by surrogate pairs, and these extended *kanji* characters has been used for Japanese person names before the age of electronics. For example, '𠮷' (U+20BB7) is very similar to basic *kanji* '吉' (U+5409), and '𠀋' (U+2000B) is similar to basic *kanji* '丈' (U+4E08), but many computer systems cannot print out the extended *kanji* characters in Supplementary Ideographic Plane. Then, Wikipedia titles a page for a proboxer to "辰吉丈一郎" instead of his proper name "辰𠮷𠀋一郎", and then guides us to the page[8], even if we, on top of Wikipedia, search a page with the proper name "辰𠮷𠀋一郎". We must take care of extended *kanji* characters with surrogate pairs in data resources.

#### 3.1.3 URI vs. IRI

N-Triples[9] is a line-based, plain text format for encoding an RDF graph, but the character encoding

[3]https://github.com/dbpedia/extraction-framework/wiki/The-DBpedia-Information-Extraction-Framework#graphsyntax

[4]http://www.w3.org/TR/rdf-syntax-grammar/

[5]http://www.w3.org/TR/rdf-mt/

[6]http://en.wikipedia.org/wiki/Semantic_Web_Stack

[7]http://www.w3.org/TR/rdf-mt/

[8]http://ja.wikipedia.org/wiki/辰吉丈一郎

[9]http://www.w3.org/TR/rdf-testcases/#ntriples

in string is designated to 7-bit US-ASCII. So, non-ASCII characters must be made available by \-escape sequences, such as '\u3042' for Japanese *hiragana* 'あ' (U+3042).[10]

RDF/XML syntax[11] designates %-encoding for disallowable characters that do not correspond to permitted US-ASCII in URI encoding, in spite that the UNICODE string as UTF-8 is designated to the RDF/XML representation. Therefore, the disallowed URL `http://ja.dbpedia.org/page/辰吉丈一郎` must be escaped as `http://ja.dbpedia.org/page/%E8%BE%B0%E5%90%89%E4%B8%88%E4%B8%80%E9%83%8E` in RDF/XML syntax.

Turtle[12] and JSON-LD[13] allow IRIs. We expect every platform for Semantic Web and LOD can process format files of Turtle and JSON-LD, and then the revised edition of RDF/XML will allow IRIs in near future.

At the end, we will be able to choose URIs if we focus on the international usability of the data, or IRIs if we take care of domestic understandability. The RFC3986, the standard of URI, says for the design of URI, "a URI often has to be remembered by people, and it is easier for people to remember a URI when it consists of meaningful or familiar components." This statement can be rephrased with replacing IRI for URI.

### 3.2 RDFization of English WordNet

The WordNet (Fellbaum, 1998) is a collection of sets of synonymous words or synsets, in which each synset, a set of synonymous words, is associated with semantic properties and values such as hypernym, hyponym, holonym, meronym, etc.

In 2006, W3C issued W3C Working Draft on RDF/OWL Representation of WordNet (van Assem, et al., 2006a), and then the authors of the draft actually made the conversion of WordNet to the RDF/OWL representation language for WordNet 2.0 (van Assem, et al., 2006b).

In the data files of English WordNet, each line of synsets includes the synonymous words with a *sense number* associated to the polysemous word for this sense. Thus, the W3C Working Draft of WordNet reflects this many to many relation between synsets and polysemous words by setting word senses.

[10] *Hiragana* are characters that represent Japanese syllables. A syllable is composed of a consonant plus a vowel.

[11] `http://www.w3.org/TR/REC-rdf-syntax/`

[12] `http://www.w3.org/TR/turtle/`

[13] `http://www.w3.org/TR/json-ld/`

After the W3C proposal for OWL conversion of WordNet, the Princeton WordNet was updated to version 2.1, in which new relations of instanceHypernym and instanceHyponym has been introduced, and now the latest version is 3.0. In following the updates of WordNet, the RDF schema for WordNet 2.0 should be reused to 2.1 and 3.0, according to one of rules for the best practice in LOD. Only for two new properties, `wn21schema:instanceHyponymOf` and `wn21schema:instanceHypernymOf` should be defined in WordNet 2.1. On the other hand, the namespaces of every instance of words, word senses, and synsets may be updated to `wn21instances` or `wn30instances`, depending on the version numbers in order to distinguish the version of data, even if the content of an entry was not updated in a new version.

### 3.3 RDFization of Japanese WordNet

The latest Japanese WordNet is built on top of Princeton's English WordNet 3.0 by adding appropriate Japanese words to the content of Princeton WordNet 3.0 on the framework of the WordNet. A polysemous Japanese word is related to more than one English synset via Japanese word senses as usual in the WordNet manner. Thus, we set up the namespace for Japanese WordNet to `wnjallinstances`. According to the W3C proposal for OWL conversion of WordNet, we converted Japanese WordNet to OWL. Here, `wnjallinstances:word-犬` (dog) is made and linked to both `wnjallinstances:wordsense-犬-noun-1` and `wnjallinstances:wordsense-犬-noun-2`. Furthermore, the former is linked to `wnjallinstances:synset-spy-noun-1` and the latter is linked to `wnjallinstances:synset-dog-noun-1`. Japanese word "犬" means "dog" and "spy", but does not mean "frump" in English. However, because of depending on the English WordNet framework, the Japanese vocabulary is not comprehensive yet, and Japanese specific concepts are still not completed.

### 3.4 Linking Japanese WordNet to DBpedia Japanese

Since both English WordNet and English Wikipedia are the most famous comprehensive language resources, there are many studies how the combination contributes to build better language resources. We have also investigated how Wikipedia Japanese can enrich Japanese

WordNet. The result of investigation suggests that it is not easy to build clean hypernym/hyponym relationship by merging two ontologies that are independently built. We think the reason is partly from inaccurate ontology buildings of the Japanese WordNet Developers, and partly from immature methodology of ontology building.

English WordNet itself includes ontological ambiguity between concepts and instances. For instance, `synset-European_Central_Bank-noun-1` is not linked via `instanceHyponymOf` but linked via `hyponymOf` to `synset-central_bank-noun-1`, although *European Central Bank* is regarded as an instance of concept *central bank* from the ontological view. *White House* as an *executive department* of American government is also not defined as instance of *executive department* but *White House* as *residence* is defined as an instance of *residence*. These facts suggest that English WordNet adopts some tacit knowledge of instances and classes. However, there is no explicit explanation about it, and it is not common in the community of ontology. Thus, we have no accurate and rational method on a firm foundation to merge WordNet to another ontology, whereas we have several similarity-based studies on ontology merging. They show much room for improvement. On the other hand, it is well known that DBpedia and its terms in the infoboxes are not sufficient to conceive of the infoboxes as ontology.

Therefore, we have here simply linked entities between Japanese WordNet and DBpedia Japanese not ontologically but literally, i.e., we link word noun entities of WordNet to DBpedia resources using property `skos:closeMatch`, where words in WordNet and resource names in Wikipedia share the same strings. Starting at the literal connection, the way of re-arranging and merging two ontologies will be studied step by step in bottom-up style, from lexicality to meaning, morphology to semantics, and linguistics to ontologies.

In linking Japanese WordNet to DBpedia Japanese, we decided to use only nouns of Japanese WordNet. One reason is that most resources in DBpedia are categorized as nouns, whereas there are categorically three types of IRIs in DBpedia, i.e., resource, property, and page of Wikipedia. Therefore, we selected resource IRIs for candidates of linking.

Table 1: WN-ja Link Number to DBpedia-ja

| DBpedia | # links | # WN nouns | rate |
|---|---|---|---|
| resources | 33,636 | 65,788 | 51.1% |

Table 2: DBpedia-ja Link Number to WN-ja

| DBpedia | # of links | # of IRIs | rate |
|---|---|---|---|
| resources | 33,636 | 1,395,329 | 2.4% |

The other reason is to avoid needless ambiguity. Japanese verbs are categorized into several types of conjugate forms. One type verb is composed of one or more (typically two) *kanji* characters (root) + "する" (conjugational suffix) for positive[14], e.g., "散歩する" (stroll), etc. Then, these roots are mostly nouns. It is obvious that a Japanese noun and a Japanese verb that shares morphemic root with the noun should be discriminated. However, Japanese WordNet does not distinguish them and then marks part-of-speech 'verb' to morphemic roots. Thus, word "散歩" is marked as noun and verb. This ambiguity will create needless links, if we link verbs in Japanese WordNet to DBpedia in addition to nouns.

Table 1 shows the statistics of linking data of Japanese WordNet to DBpedia Japanese, and Table 2 shows the statistics of linking data of DBpedia Japanese to Japanese WordNet. The lexically exact mapping produces one by one and inversely equivalent matching between both.

## 4 RDFization of IPAdic and Links to DBpedia Japanese

### 4.1 OWL Conversion of IPAdic

In the RDFization of IPAdic 2.7.0, we encountered one typical problem in RDF, that is, the domain and range problem. Every property in RDF restricts the class of its subject and object of a given triple in a context. For instance, a property of `wn20schema:sense` designates an instance of `wn20schema:Word` for subject and an instance of `wn20schema:WordSense` for object, and vice versa on `wn20schema:word`. In the conversion of IPAdic, the adoption of properties defined in WordNet 2.0 schema will result in forcing the classification to WordNet classes on IPAdic entries. Therefore, we newly defined a schema, in which properties of IPAdic which

[14]and + "しない" for negative

are similar to WordNet but whose namespace is different from WordNet.[15] In other words, we, instead of `wn20schema:word` and `wn20schema:sense`, defined and used `ipadic27schema:word` and `ipadic27schema:sense`, of which the domain and range are `ipadic27schema:Word` and `ipadic27schema:WordSense`.

In addition, we reflected the information of parts of speech, connection costs, lemmas, and word readings of IPAdic into the schema. In this RDFization process, we recognized that a lemma and a reading represented by *katakana*[16] for a *kanji* word should be assigned to a sense but not the word. Thus, we defined the domain of `ipadic27schema:reading` as `ipadic27schema:WordSense` in order to reflect such Japanese sense structure in IPAdic, whereas there is no description of senses or means. We generated entities of word senses from words in order to enable the assignment of lemmas and readings to them.

### 4.2 Linking IPAdic to DBpedia Japanese

The outcomes of the conversion of IPAdic are linked to DBpedia Japanese with literal matching between noun words in IPAdic and resource names of DBpedia. In spite of the creation of word senses in the IPAdic, the connection of IPAdic entries as sense is suppressed, because there is no explicit evidence on senses in IPAdic for connecting to DBpedia Japanese. The connection from word senses of IPAdic to DBpedia is left as work in near future.

Table 3 shows the number of links and the rate from IPAdic to DBpedia Japanese, and Table 4 for the number of links and the rate from DBpedia Japanese to IPAdic.

Table 3: IPAdict Link Number to DBpedia-ja

| DBpedia | # linked | # IPAdic nouns | rate |
|---|---|---|---|
| resources | 54,735 | 197,479 | 27.7% |

## 5 Publishing as LOD

As a means of registration at the Data Hub[17], DBpedia Japanese has been published as the Japanese hub of LOD with CC-BY-SA license. It is available from our site[18] to access the data *dereferenceablly*, make a query at a SPARQL endpoint, and dump the zip files. This DBpedia Japanese includes the links to Japanese WordNet in lexical level.

Table 4: DBpedia-ja Link Number to IPAdic

| DBpedia | # linked | # IRIs | rate |
|---|---|---|---|
| resources | 54,735 | 1,456,158 | 3.8% |

Japanese WordNet and IPAdic have also been published under a CC-BY-SA license, same as DBpedia Japanese, from our sites.[19] The dump files are also available at our repository. [20]

It is critical as LOD to make all entities *dereferenceable*. We acquired the domain names wordnet.jp and ipadic.jp to obtain controllable domain names for Japanese WordNet and IPAdic, and then SPARQL endpoints are opened with `http://wordnet.jp/` and `http://ipadic.jp/` in addition of making the entries *dereferenceable*.

## 6 Related Work

As described so far in this paper, this work is the first attempt of LOD on Japanese linguistic resources. However, several studies in Semantic Webs related to dictionaries and ontologies have been completed before the advent of LOD. Koide, et al. (2006) performed OWL conversion of EDR and Princeton WordNet 2.1 according to the W3C working draft on OWL conversion. The converted files were open and down-loadable but there was no *dereferenceable* web site and no SPARQL endpoint, as things in the pre-LOD age.

An LOD site for words and characters in multilinguistics were opend by de Melo and Weikum (2008).

YAGO (Suchanek, et al., 2008) is the first substantial study of automatic ontology construction from two comprehensive English resources, Wikipedia and WordNet. YAGO conceives of Wikipedia as knowledge about facts. Then, a semantic model like RDFS, which is closed within DBpeida (called YAGO model),[21] is used for capturing facts in DBpedia with reifying the fact.

[15] Truly, we can set only classes and properties newly required, and add them to an existing set of WordNet properties, since RDF semantics allows that an instance is classified into multiple classes. However, it will be easy to cause misunderstanding and misusage by users.

[16] *Katakana* is a Japanese syllabary like *hiragana* but it is ofen used to represent loanwords and imitative words.

[17] `http://datahub.io/`

[18] `http://ja.dbpedia.org/`

[19] `http://wordnet.jp/` and `http://ipadic.jp/`

[20] `http://lod.ac/dumps/wordnet/20130724/` and `http://lod.ac/dumps/wordnet/20130724/`

[21] The elemental model in Semantic Webs must be open.

Each synset of WordNet becomes a class of YAGO. The Wikipedia category hierarchy is abandoned, and only the leaves are used for the factual information extraction. The lower classes extracted from Wikipedia conceptual category are connected to higher classes extracted from WordNet. Therefore, YAGO takes care of the quality of types of individuals and there is no way to improve the ontology of WordNet. The automatic ontology construction in higher classes and the merging of multiple-ontologies that may contain inconsistency is still an open problem.

Ontology alignment is critical to obtain one united resource from two inconsistent resources with different coverages, different ontological structures, and different semantics. There are many studies on ontology alignment up to now.[22] However, these studies show immaturity on science and methodology of ontology building. Currently, similarity of lexical texts, synonym sets, and hypernym/hyponym tree structure is only a way to merge multiple linguistic resources. Hayashi (2012) proposed a new method to compute cross-lingual semantic similarity using synonym sets.

## 7 Conclusion and Feature Work

In this paper, we described the practice, reality, and difficulty of RDFization on two distinct Japanese dictionaries, Japanese WordNet and IPAdic, together with the benefit of and the expectation to LLOD. In this LLOD attempt, the linkage is realized on the surface level of lexicality. The linkage between word senses of WordNet and disambiguated DBpedia resources will be studied in near future, and the connection from word senses of IPAdic to DBpedia, too.

The power of LOD resides in the nature of openness and commonality. Thus, LLOD is the nature of linguistics because of the commonality of linguistics. We believe that the outcomes of LLOD will be infrastructure in each society of countries and the international world in future.

## References


C. Bizer, J. Lehmann, G. Kobilarov, S. Auer, C. Becker, R. Cyganiak, and S. Hellmann. 2009. DBpedia - A Crystallization Point for the Web of Data, *J. Web Semantics*, 7(3):154–165.

Gerard de Melo, Gerhard Weikum. 2008. Language as a Foundation of the Semantic Web, 7th International Semantic Web Conference (ISWC2008), Poster.

Yasuharu Den, Junpei Nakamura, Toshinobu Ogiso, Hideki Ogura. 2008. A proper approach to Japanese morphological analysis: Dictionary, model, and evaluation, *The 6th Edition of Language Resources and Evaluation Conference* (LREC-2008), Marrakech.

Christiane Fellbaum (ed.). 1998. *WordNet: An Electronic Lexical Database*. MIT Press.

Yoshihiko Hayashi. 2013. Computing Cross-Lingual Synonym Set Similarity by Using Princeton Annotated Gloss Corpus, *Proc. Global Wordnet Conf.*(GWC2012), Matsue, 134–141 Tribun EU.

Tom Heath and Christian Bizer. 2011. *Linked Data: Evolving the Web into a Global Data Space*, Morgan & Claypool.

Satoru Ikehara, et al. 1997. *Goi-Taikei — A Japanese Lexicon*, Iwanami Shoten, Tokyo.

Hitoshi Isahara, Francis Bond, Kiyotaka Uchimoto, Masao Utiyama, and Kyoko Kanzaki. 2008. Development of Japanese WordNet, *The 6th Edition of the Language Resources and Evaluation Conference* (LREC-2008), Marrakech.

Seiji Koide, Takeshi Morita, Takahira Yamaguchi, Hendry Muljadi, Hideaki Takeda. 2006. RDF/OWL Representation of WordNet 2.1 and Japanese EDR Electric Dictionary, 5th International Semantic Web Conference (ISWC2006), Poster.

Yuji Matsumoto, Akira Kitauchi, Tatsuo Yamashita, and Yoshitaka Hirano. 1999. *Japanese Morphological Analysis System ChaSen version 2.0 Manual*, NAIST Technical Report, NAIST-IS-TR99009.

Fabian M. Suchanek, Gjergji Kasneci, Gerhard Weikum. 2008. YAGO: A Large Ontology from Wikipedia and WordNet, *Web Semantics: Science, Services and Agents on the World Wide Web*, 6:203–217, Elsevier.

Mark van Assem, Aldo Gangemi, and Guus Schreiber. 2006. RDF/OWL Representation of WordNet, W3C Working Draft, `http://www.w3.org/TR/wordnet-rdf/`.

Mark van Assem, Aldo Gangemi, and Guus Schreiber. 2006. Conversion of WordNet to a standard RDF/OWL representation, Proc. (LREC-2006).

Toshio Yokoi. 1995. The EDR Electronic Dictionary, *Commun. ACM*, 38(11):42–44.


[22]See `http://ontologymatching.org/publications.html`

# Migrating Psycholinguistic Semantic Feature Norms into Linked Data in Linguistics

**Yoshihiko Hayashi**
Graduate School of Language and Culture, Osaka University
1-8 Machikaneyma, Toyonaka 5600043, Japan
hayashi@lang.osaka-u.ac.jp

## Abstract

Semantic feature norms, originally utilized in the field of psycholinguistics as a tool for studying human semantic representation and computation, have recently attracted the attention of some NLP/IR researchers who wish to improve their task performances. However, currently available semantic feature norms are, by nature, not well-structured, making them difficult to integrate into existing resources of various kinds. In this paper, by examining an actual set of semantic feature norms, we investigate which types of semantic features should be migrated into Linked Data in Linguistics (LDL) and how the migration could be done.

## 1 Introduction

Recently, some NLP/IR researchers have become interested in incorporating psycholinguistic features into their applications to improve task performance (Kwong, 2012; Tanaka et al., 2013). Among a range of psycholinguistic features, such as imageability, concreteness, and familiarity (Paivio et al., 1968), the most attractive is a set of semantic feature norms introduced by McRae et al. (2005). It captures prominent associative knowledge about a concept possessed by humans. Silberer and Lapata (2012), for example, employ semantic feature norms as a proxy for human sensorimotor experiences in their semantic representation model, and report improved performance in word association and word similarity computation tasks. However, currently available semantic feature norms are, by nature, not well-structured, making them difficult to integrate into existing resources of various kinds.

Given this background, in this paper, we extract a tentative set of *psycholinguistically significant* semantic feature types, and draw a technical map to structurize corresponding semantic feature norms by observing the Linked Data paradigm. Note that psycholinguistically significant semantic feature types, in particular, dictate semantic relations that amply observe associations by humans; however, those are usually *not* considered in existing lexico-ontological resources.

| Semantic feature | BR Label |
|---|---|
| `a_reptile` | *taxonomic* |
| `beh_-_eats_people` | *visual-motion* |
| `beh_-_swims` | *visual-motion* |
| `has_a_mouth` | *visual-form_and_surface* |
| `has_jaws` | *visual-form_and_surface* |
| `has_scales` | *visual-form_and_surface* |
| `is_dangerous` | *encyclopaedic* |
| `is_long` | *visual-form_and_surface* |
| `lives_in_swamps` | *encyclopaedic* |

Table 1: Semantic feature norms and the BR Labels for describing `alligator`.

## 2 Semantic Feature Norms

### 2.1 Overview of McRae's Database

In this paper, we take the well-known set of semantic feature norms provided by McRae et al. (2005) (henceforth, McRae's database) as an actual example. This database provides a total of 7,526 semantic feature norms assigned to 541 living and nonliving basic-level concepts, each organized on the basis of experimental data collected from a large number of participants. McRae's database also presents a range of supplementary information, including statistical data about the semantic features.

Table 1 displays some of the semantic feature norms given to describe `alligator`. Although not fully shown in the table, more than ten features are used to describe several aspects of `alligator`. In Table 1, Brain Region (BR) Labels are also shown, each of which roughly classifies semantic features from the perspective of brain function localization (Cree and McRae, 2003). See Appendix-A for more details.

### 2.2 Semantic Feature Keywords

As exemplified in Table 1, all of the semantic features are prefixed by predefined keywords or key phrases (e.g., `beh_-` in "`beh_-` eats_people"; "`lives_in` swamps"). These keywords and key phrases (henceforth, semantic-feature keywords) can be utilized to classify semantic features into basic types.

| Semantic-feature keyword | # of variations |
|---|---|
| used_for | 469 |
| has | 257 |
| is | 247 |
| has_a | 192 |
| a | 139 |
| beh_- | 138 |
| used_by | 113 |
| made_of | 70 |
| requires | 66 |
| inbeh_- | 64 |
| lives_in | 57 |
| found_in | 52 |
| associated_with | 44 |
| worn_for | 43 |
| eg_- | 40 |

Table 2: Productive semantic-feature keywords.

Although McRae et al. (2005) described around twenty semantic-feature keywords, the database actually classifies almost one hundred semantic-feature keywords, including presumably erroneous ones. Table 2 lists fifteen of the most productive semantic-feature keywords, in the sense of how many variations they have in the semantic feature norm instances. Most of the semantic feature keywords are self-descriptive; however, note that `beh_-` signifies behavior exhibited by animate beings (e.g., "`alligator beh_-` eats_people"), while `inbeh_-` denotes that an inanimate being does something seemingly on its own (e.g., "`airplane inbeh_-` crashes").

## 3 Structurizing Semantic Feature Norms

Figure 1, which corresponds to the `alligator` example shown in Table 1, illustrates a fundamental method of structurizing the semantic feature norms in McRae's database into a Linked Data graph[1]. The graph is constructed as follows: (1) A subject node is created for the target concept; (2) the subject node is linked with a set of triple objects, each representing a semantic feature; (3) a residual feature expression[2] is analyzed where necessary; and (4) each of the triple predicates carries a corresponding semantic feature type. In addition, the constructs of the graph should be linked with existing external Linked Data constructs whenever possible. In Fig. 1, word nodes are assumed to be linked with corresponding WordNet synset nodes by semantically disambiguating them. We may further need to resolve named entities, if we are to link them, for example, with DBPedia nodes.

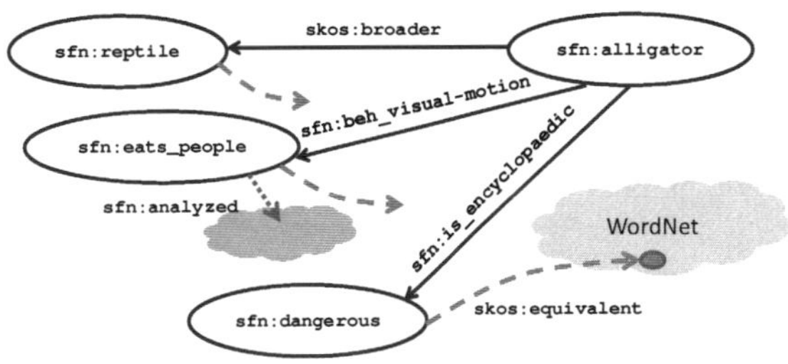


Figure 1: Linked Data graph structurizing a set of semantic features.

To actualize this illustration, we first need to create an inventory of triple predicates by identifying a reasonable set of semantic feature types, and then derive the sub-types where necessary.

## 4 Case Studies

We conducted our investigations by first extracting the tentative set of psycholinguistically significant semantic feature types shown in Table 3 from the ones already listed in Table 2 by performing the following actions:

- Excluding semantic feature types thought to be typical ontological constructs: these include, hyponymy (`a`), meronymy (`has_a, made_of, part_of`), telic/functional (`used_for, used_by`), exemplary (`eg_-`), causal (`causes`), and their subtypes (e.g., `worn_for`).
- Putting off semantic feature types whose semantics are clear and relatively restricted, such as `lives_in` and `found_in`, which both specify concrete/abstract places.

[1] In this paper, `sfn` denotes an imaginary prefix for representing constructs of a Linked Data graph. A more detailed modeling example using *lemon* (McCrae et al., 2010) is shown in Appendix-B.

[2] A *residual feature expression* denotes the natural language expression that follows a semantic-feature keyword: for example, "eats people" in "`alligator beh_-` eats people."

| Semantic feature type | Example feature expressions |
| --- | --- |
| associated_with | cape associated_with Batman |
| is | apple is crunchy |
| requires | bread requires baking |
| beh_ - | alligator beh_- eats_people |
| inbeh_- | airplane inbeh_- crashes |

Table 3: Psycholinguistically significant semantic feature types (tentative).

| BR Label | Token frequency |
| --- | --- |
| *visual-form_and_surface* | 546 |
| *visual-color* | 350 |
| *encyclopaedic* | 111 |
| *tactile* | 238 |
| *function* | 108 |
| *visual-motion* | 40 |
| *sound* | 34 |
| *smell* | 20 |

Table 4: Distribution of BR Labels for `is`.

The following subsections examine these nominated semantic feature types in turn.

### 4.1 `associated_with`

The "associated_with" semantic feature type associates a target concept with something associated with it, without specifying any particular semantic restrictions. The fact that all of the instances are labeled with *encyclopaedic* BR Labels endorses this action. Furthermore, this semantic-feature keyword exhibits a very high type/token ratio (TTR) of 0.96, asserting that an associated object is highly specific to the target concept, as exemplified by the "Batman" example shown in Table 3. Recall here that a type refers to a distinct semantic feature expression (word/phrase) succeeding a semantic-feature keyword, while a token dictates an occurrence of a semantic feature expression type.

The only thing we can do to structurize this semantic feature type is introduce a triple predicate such as, `sfn:associated_with`, as asserted in the above discussion.

### 4.2 `is`

The "is" semantic feature type in essence dictates several aspects/characteristics of a target concept from a variety of perspectives. In contrast to `associated_with`, this semantic feature type computed a very low TTR of 0.15: where the number of feature expression types was 247, while that of tokens amounted to 1,651. This situation forced us to further classify the feature expression types.

Here, we propose to classify this semantic feature type into a subclass by referring to the BR Labels. For example, by introducing the corresponding BR Label, "`alligator is` long" can be triplized as follows:

```
sfn:alligator
    sfn:is_visual-form_and_surface
sfn:long .
```

Table 4 summarizes the distribution of BR Labels for the `is` semantic feature type, where all but *function* and *encyclopaedic* are perceptual categories.

### 4.3 `requires`

The "requires" semantic feature type primarily specifies a typical object or entity that is somehow required by a nonliving target concept[3]. In contrast to the `is` semantic feature type, we cannot introduce BR Labels to further classify this semantic feature type into a subclass, as many of them (80/93 = 86.0%) are annotated with *encyclopaedic*, and the rest with *function*.

Therefore, we decided to investigate the semantic types of the *required* things by ourselves, and induced a set of sub-categories to combine with `requires`. Table 5 lists the sub-categories and the corresponding instance frequencies. Note that we in essence adopted semantic criteria from the Princeton WordNet for distinguishing physical/abstract entities: We however added *human* and *operation* to adequately classify the required things. With this in mind, "`bread requires` baking," for example, can be triplized as follows:

```
sfn:bread
    sfn:requires_operation
sfn:baking .
```

### 4.4 `beh_-/inbeh_-`

The "beh-" and "inbeh-" semantic feature types should intrinsically be considered *meta* feature types, only signaling typical or salient behavior/movement described in the residual feature expression, as seen in the examples introduced above: "`alligator beh_-` eats people" and "`airplane inbeh_-` crashes." Furthermore, as each of these expressions, in general, form a verb phrase, we would need to linguistically analyze the verb phrase to extract its semantic content.

[3]We observed 93 instances of the `requires` type in McRae's database, of which only two described living things.

| Semantic type | Token frequency | Example feature expression |
|---|---|---|
| physical entity | 55 | `balloon requires` helium |
| human | 19 | `bus requires` driver |
| operation | 13 | `bread requires` baking |
| abstract entity | 6 | `unicycle requires` balance |

Table 5: Semantic types of *required* things.

| Types | *encyclopedia* | *sound* | *visual-motion* |
|---|---|---|---|
| `beh_-` | 95 | 56 | 267 |
| `inbeh_-` | 33 | 50 | 32 |

Table 6: Distribution of BR Labels for `beh/inbeh`.

Further specification of such a linguistic analysis and the representation of the analysis results, however, are beyond the scope of this paper. We here focus instead on the sub-typing of these semantic feature types. As done earlier, we first checked the TTRs: `beh_-` computed 0.33, while `inbeh_-` exhibited 0.55, showing that some of the semantic-feature expression types are moderately productive. We then checked the distribution of the BR Labels, shown in Table 6[4]. The table clearly shows that only a few BR Labels are actually employed. Therefore, we decided to combine the BR Labels with these meta semantic feature types. Following this rationale, "`alligator beh_-_` eats people," for example, can be triplized as follows:

```
sfn:alligator
    sfn:beh_visual-motion
sfn:eats_people .
```

Intriguingly, while the majority of the behaviors taken by animate beings (`beh`-type) are classified as *visual-motion* (267/419 = 63.7%), the behaviors taken by inanimate beings (`inbeh`-type) are distributed across three categories: *encyclopaedic*, *sound*, and *visual-motion*, implying that the visibility of a behavior plays a psychologically prominent role in the characterization of living things.

## 5 Discussion

Psycholinguistic semantic features, in general, can improve the performance of semantic tasks in NLP, as demonstrated by Silberer and Lapata (2012). In other words, semantic features that are focused more on human perception should be combined with linguistic features. In this sense, migration of psycholinguistic semantic feature norms into a Linked Data cloud could provide an opportunity for a range of NLP applications to exploit psycholinguistic semantic features in combination with linguistic features acquirable from existing lexico-ontological resources.

The true benefits to be derived from publishing them as Linked Data, in particular, should be underpinned by concrete NLP applications. They are unfortunately not very clear at the moment, but the key to success is to employ the structurized set of psycholinguistic semantic features as a gateway to accessing existing resources of various kinds: including not only lexical/encyclopaedic resources such as WordNet, Wiktionary, and DBPedia, but also domain-specific ontologies such as GeoSpecies[5]. In this scenario, enabling proper linking with external resources is quite important.

Another crucial issue that has to be addressed in order to achieve the goal is the fact that the coverage of semantic feature norms needs to be significantly widened because currently available psycholinguistic resources, such as McRae's database, provide semantic features only for a limited number of concepts, notably, concrete concepts. Therefore, the development of a method to infer semantic features even for concepts not yet covered by existing resources (Johns and Jones, 2012) or, more importantly, a mechanism to mine useful properties from corpora (Baroni et al., 2010) would be highly appreciated.

## 6 Concluding Remarks

By examining the well-known McRae's database (McRae et al., 2005), we organized a reasonable set of psycholinguistically significant semantic feature types, and sketched a scenario for migrating them into the LDL.

For short-to-medium-term future work, we plan to (1) investigate other less-frequent/less-prominent semantic features observed in McRae's database; and (2) implement a computational process to actually convert the semantic feature norms into a set of Linked Data graphs.

[4]Labels with less than two occurrences have been omitted.

[5]`http://lod.geospecies.org/`

## Acknowledgments

This work was supported by JSPS KAKENHI Grant Number 258201170.

## References

Marco Baroni, Brian Murphy, Eduard Barbu, and Massimo Poesio. 2010. Strudel: A corpus-based semantic model based on properties and types. *Cognitive Science*, 34:222–254.

George S. Cree and Ken McRae. 2003. Analyzing the factors underlying the structure and computation of the meaning of chipmunk, cherry, chisel, cheese, and cello (and many other such concrete nouns). *Journal of Experimental Psychology*, 132:163–201.

Bredan T. Johns and Michael N. Jones. 2012. Perceptual inference through global lexical similarity. *Topics in Cognitive Science*, 4:103–120.

Oi Yee Kwong. 2012. *New Perspectives on Computational and Cognitive Strategies for Word Sense Disambiguation*, Springer.

John McCrae, et al. 2010. The *lemon* cookbook, `http://lexinfo.net/lemon-cookbook.pdf`

John McCrae, Elena Montiel-Ponsoda, and Philipp Cimiano. 2012. Integrating WordNet and Wiktionary with *lemon*, In Chiristian Chiarcos et al. (eds.) *Linked Data in Linguistics*, Springer-Verlag, pp.25–29.

Ken McRae, George S. Cree, and Mark S. Seidenberg. 2005. Semantic feature production norms for a large set of living and nonliving things, *Behaviour Research Methods, Instruments, and Computers*, 37(4):547–559.

Allan Paivio, John C. Yuille, and Stephen A. Madigan. 1968. Concreteness, imagery, and meaningfulness values for 925 nouns, *Journal of Experimental Psychology*, 76 (1, Part 2):1–25.

Carina Silberer and Mirella Lapata. 2012. Grounded models of semantic representation, *Proceedings of the 2012 Joint Conference on EMNLP*, pp.1423–1433.

Sinya Tanaka, Adam Jatowt, Makoto P. Kato, and Katsumi Tanaka. 2013. Estimating content concreteness for finding comprehensible documents, *Proceedings of The Sixth ACM WSDM Conference*, pp.475–484.

## Appendix-A: Brain Region Labels

Each of the BR Labels assigned to a semantic feature norm in the database is based on a taxonomy called *Brain Region Taxonomy* (Cree and McRae, 2003). Table A-1 classifies the nine (plus one: *taxonomic*) categories defined by the BR taxonomy, and the corresponding token frequencies in the database. Cree and McRae (2003) argue that these categories represent knowledge types that are closely associated with corresponding brain regions.

| BR Label | Frequency |
|---|---|
| *visual-form-and-surface* | 2,336 |
| *visual-color* | 424 |
| *visual-motion* | 339 |
| *tactile* | 245 |
| *sound* | 142 |
| *taste* | 84 |
| *smell* | 24 |
| *function* | 1,517 |
| *encyclopaedic* | 1,417 |
| *taxonomic* | 730 |

Table A-1: Distribution of the BR Labels.

As displayed in Table A-1, seven of the nine categories are linked with sensory channels/modes, of which three are associated with visual perception. In particular, the category *visual-form-and-surface* exhibits substantially high frequency, highlighting the fact that *visibility* plays a significant role in characterizing a concrete object psycholinguistically. The category *function*, on the other hand, organizes feature types, such as `used_for` and `used_by`, describing functional aspects of a target concept. Semantic features encoding other types of miscellaneous knowledge were labeled as *encyclopaedic*.

## Appendix-B: Modeling with *lemon*

Figure B-1 exemplifies a more detailed modeling of the Linked Data graph presented in Fig. 1. In this modeling, McRae's entire database is modeled as a *lemon* lexicon. That is, every content word in McRae's database is modeled as a lexical entry, and the semantic feature types, derived in this paper, are modeled as sub-properties of `lemon:senseRelation`, which connects `lemon:sense` instances. In addition, linking to WordNet is represented by using `lemon:reference`, as in (McCrae et al., 2012), meaning that WordNet is treated as an external ontological resource.

Notice also that the residual semantic feature expression, such as "eats people," is modeled as a phrasal lexical entry, whose internal linguistic structure is meanwhile represented by a syntactic dependency structure, represented by the blue cloud in the figure.

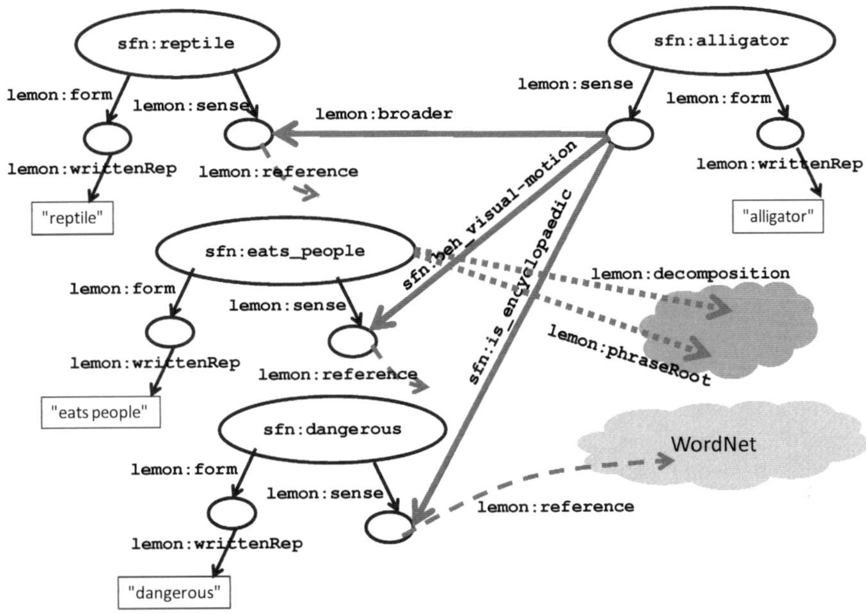


Figure B-1: Modeling using *lemon*.

# Towards the establishment of a linguistic linked data network for Italian

**Roberto Bartolini**
ILC - CNR
Via Moruzzi 1 - Pisa, Italy

**Riccardo Del Gratta**
ILC - CNR
Via Moruzzi 1 - Pisa, Italy

**Francesca Frontini**
ILC - CNR
Via Moruzzi 1 - Pisa, Italy

name.surname@ilc.cnr.it

### Abstract

This paper describes the conversion of ItalwordNet and of a domain WordNet into RDF and their linking to the (L)LOD cloud and to other existing resources. A brief presentation of the resources is given, and the conversion and resulting datasets are described.

## 1 Introduction

Lexical Resources, both manually and automatically created, are an indispensable component to many NLP applications. In order to make lexical resources more accessible, the importance of adhering to common models has always been underlined, and in the course of time standards and best practices for the representation of such resources have emerged.

With the rise of the Semantic Web, efforts that aimed to provide common annotation and sharing formats to make resources more interoperable have found a new ally in the linked data paradigm (Berners-Lee, 2006), which generally pairs with the adoption of the RDF formalism (Lassila and Swick, 1999).

Indeed a new trend in the publication of linguistic resources as linked open data seems to be establishing itself: a survey on the formats and frameworks used in the last 20 years to exchange linguistic resources, (Lezcano et al., 2013) found "an increase in recent years in approaches adopting the Linked Data initiative".

Although still quantitatively a minority within the linked data cloud, (Linguistic) Linked Open Data ((L)LOD)[1], (Chiarcos et al., 2011; Chiarcos, 2012), is growing and becoming a central modality for linguistic data and especially for lexical data publication. Lexicographic data may not always be big in number of triples, but they are significant in specific weight - especially the resources manually developed/checked, as they contain complex semantic information that has been encoded by humans.

Following the path of this movement, the publication of lexical resources in the Italian language has also started.

In this paper a description of the conversion of ItalwordNet and of a WordNet in the geographic domain is given.

## 2 Resource used for establishing a linguistic linked data network for Italian

### 2.1 PAROLE SIMPLE CLIPS

PAROLE SIMPLE CLIPS is a multi-layered Italian language lexicon that was the outcome of three major lexical resource projects: PAROLE (Ruimy et al., 1998) and SIMPLE (Lenci et al., 2000), two consecutive European projects, and CLIPS , an Italian national project which enlarged and refined the Italian PAROLE-SIMPLE lexicon.

The lexical information in PAROLE SIMPLE CLIPS is encoded at different descriptive levels; these are the phonetic, morphological, syntactic and semantic layers. The semantic layer of PAROLE SIMPLE CLIPS (PSC), SIMPLE, is largely based on Pustejovsky's Generative Lexicon (GL) theory (Pustejovsky, 1991; Bel et al., 2000). This level contains a language independent ontology of 153 semantic types as well as $\sim 60k$ so called "semantic units", or *Usems*, representing the meanings of lexical entries in the lexicon: more specifically, these encode the *extended qualia structure* (Ruimy et al., 2002) and provide useful information on the semantic type of a concept (formal quale), its constituent parts (constitutive quale), on how it came into being (agentive quale) and on its purpose (telic quale). SIMPLE lexicons exist for several languages and *Usems* are consistently

[1] http://linguistics.okfn.org/resources/llod/.

linked to a common Simple Interlingual Ontology (SIO) of generic concepts labeled in English.

Recently a partial publication of the Italian PSC lexicon as RDF linked data has been carried out (del Gratta et al., 2013) and provided to the community. Other SIMPLE lexicons such as the Spanish one (Villegas and Bel, 2013) are currently also publicly available in RDF. The Simple Interlingual Ontology has been formalized into OWL by (Toral and Monachini, 2007) and it is also publicly available.

### 2.2 ItalwordNet

ItalwordNet (IWN) (Roventini et al., 2003) is a semantical lexical database developed along the lines of Princeton WordNet, (Fellbaum, 2010). IWN started within the EuroWordNet[2] project as the "Italian WordNet" and then subsequently refined in different Italian projects such as SI-TAL.

The ItalwordNet resource increased thanks to manually-developed mapping, known as Inter-Lingual Index (ILI), between its synsets and synsets in different WordNets (WNs). As the name suggests, the ILI is a connection among concepts in different languages. In ItalwordNet the ILI between Italian and English synsets in WordNet 1.5, (WN1.5), has been used to connect Italian to English concepts; successively, exploiting the WN1.5 to WN3.0 mapping[3], IWN and WN3.0 have been semi-automatically linked. The formalization of IWN into RDF is finalized with a partial mapping to PSC, see figure 1.

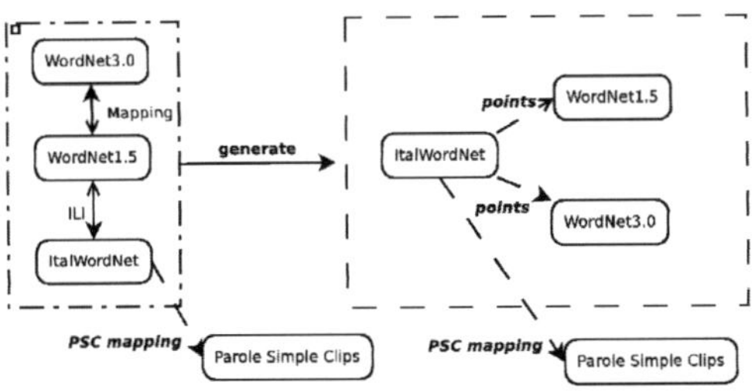


Figure 1: ILI and WordNet1.5-WN3.0 mapping expand the IWN; the mapping to PSC adds more dimensions.

[2]http://www.illc.uva.nl/EuroWordNet/.

[3]The static mapping between WordNets 1.5 and 3.0 have been downloaded from http://nlp.lsi.upc.edu/tools/download-map.php.

## 3 ItalwordNet schema and dataset description

The conversion of ItalwordNet into RDF was carried out following the strategy used to convert WN into RDF, whose rules and philosophy are reported in http://www.w3.org/TR/wordnet-rdf. This schema[4] is still the reference schema for any other WN[5] and contains all objects we need to perform the conversion.

As a consequence, the proposed schema for ItalwordNet complements the one adopted for WN2.0: the main classes (*Synset*, *WordSense* and *Word*) and subclasses[6] of WordNet have been extended to address specificities of ItalwordNet. For example, the proposed schema contains additional subclasses for both *Synset* and *WordSense* to address the *ProperNoun (NP)* part of speech which is present in the ItalwordNet only, see figure 2.

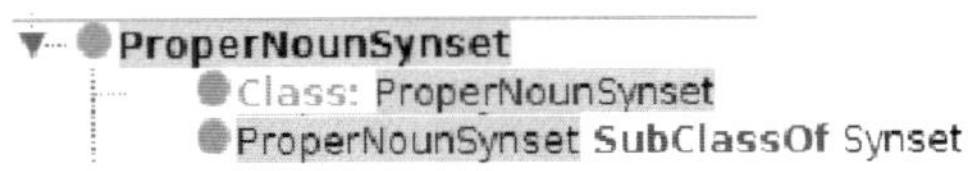


Figure 2: IWN schema is an extension of WN2.0

Similarly the set of relations in ItalwordNet is different from the one of WordNet.

Due to the specificity of the Italian language, IWN contains relations that are not defined in WN. Relations among synsets such as "involved_location" and "be_in_state" do not exist in WN2.0 but are strongly used in IWN: as a consequence, they have been defined in the IWN schema, enforcing the concept of IWN schema as a complementing schema.

Finally, the ItalwordNet schema defines relations for managing interlingual "pointers" to WNs and links to PSC. Such relations can be both *objectProperty*, used to manage the pointer(s) between IWN and the corresponding WN3.0 synset(s) and *dataProperty*, used to managed the pointer(s) between IWN and the static value of the corresponding synset(s) in WN1.5, since this resource in not available in RDF.

[4]The complete schema for WN2.0 is available at http://www.w3.org/2006/03/wn/wn20/schemas/wnfull.rdfs.

[5]Cf. http://purl.org/vocabularies/princeton/wn30/, for example.

[6]Subclasses of *Synset* and *WordSense* are related to parts of speech: *Noun (N)* part of speech generates *NounSynset* and *NounWordSense* subclasses.

The PSC mapping is managed by as *objectProperty* as well, see figure 3.

Figure 3: Object and Data properties

### 3.1 ItalwordNet Naming Convention

The unique identifiers for instances of *Synset*, *WordSense* and *Word* follow the syntactic pattern defined for WN2.0:

```
synset|wordsense-lexicalentry-pos-sense

          word-lexicalentry
```

For example, `synset-casa-noun-1` identifies the synset whose list of members contains the sense 1 of the word *casa* (home).[7] Therefore, the Uniform Resource Identifiers (URIs) for such instances are generated by combining the basic namespace (hereafter, `base`): `www.languagelibrary.eu/owl/italWordNet15` with the keyword `instances` and the corresponding class identifiers. For example:

```
base/instances/synset-casa-noun-1
```

is the URI where the synset (identified by `synset-casa-noun-1` ) is accessible. To refine the ItalwordNet resource we have defined a second namespace for its official schema[8], `iwn15schema = base/schema`, and a set of files which group the synsets according to a given relation.[9]

[7]The synset identified above contains 6 senses, including the one related to "casa", (home), that to "abitazione", (habitation) etc.. We selected "casa" (and its sense) to be the part of the human readable synset identifier.

[8]The schema is available at `base/schema/iwn`.

[9]For example, the file "has_hyponym" contains all couples of synsets which are connected by the "hyponym" relation.

### 3.2 ItalwordNet in RDF: triples

Table 1 gives the number of effective *subject-predicate-object* triples, table 2 reports some example data in terms of obtained triples for some relations and table 3 sums all triples obtained from the relations among IWN and WN synsets as well as the one from the mapping to PSC:

Table 1: Files, units and triples

| File | Original Units | Triples |
|---|---|---|
| synset | 46,769 | 148,050 |
| wordsenseandwords | 68,548 (wordsenses)<br>46,769 (words) | 367,766 |

Table 2: A sample of files and obtained triples

| Namespace | File | Triples |
|---|---|---|
| iwn15schema | has_hyponym | 44,603 |
| iwn15schema | has_meronym | 323 |
| iwn15schema | eq_synonym | 35,653 |

Table 3: Internal and external relations (`iwn15schema` namespace)

| Source resource | Triples | Target Resource |
|---|---|---|
| IWN | 132,212 | IWN |
| | 56,074 | WN1.5 |
| | 54,717 | WN3.0 |
| | 19,896 | PSC |

**IWN → IWN** Triples as *objectProperty* encoding all internal synset-synset relations in ItalwordNet;

**IWN → WN**1.5 Triples as *dataProperty* encoding ILI relations;

**IWN → WN**3.0 Triples as *objectProperty* encoding ILI relations. The domain of the relation is a IWN synset, the range is a valid WN3.0 URI;[10]

**IWN → PSC** Triples as *objectProperty* encoding the IWN PSC mapping. The domain of the relation is a IWN synse, the range is a valid PSC URI.[11]

[10]Such as http://purl.org/vocabularies/princeton/wn30/synset-chair-noun-1.

[11]such as http://www.languagelibrary.eu/owl/simple/inds/2/299/USem1450limone.

## 4 Geodomain resources

The Geodomain WNs were created within the framework of the GLOSS project (Frontini et al., 2012) in order to initialize a parallel terminology for the semantic annotation and mining of documents in the public security domain. The English resource was created by using the Geonames ontology[12], transforming each English label into a lexical entry, and then manually linking them to corresponding synsets.

Subsequently the English labels and glosses have been translated into Italian to produce an equivalent Italian resource.

### 4.1 Building a Domain WordNet

In this section we describe the strategy used to create a Domain WordNet from an human made list of domain lexical entries. The strategy follows the following steps: (i) a sense number is added to a lexical entry: in principle, we have to take care of the fact that the same lexical entry can belong to different concepts, such as for example for the lexical entry "hill" which can be both an underwater hill and a small mountain; (ii) then a referent (identifier) of the synset must be created; (iii) WordNet2.0 relations among synset are established; finally (iv) the synset previously created is connected to the concept into the Geonames ontology through the *owl:sameAs* property.

### 4.2 GeoDomainWN schema and dataset description

The conversion of GeoDomainWN into RDF was carried out following the steps described in section 3 but, at the moment, there is no need to create a dedicated schema, so that the provided resource will use the standard WN2.0 schema.

### 4.3 GeoDomainWN Naming Convention

The unique identifiers for instances of *Synset*, *WordSense* and *Word* follow the syntactic pattern defined for IWN, see section 3.1, but we have prefixed each identifier with `geo` to avoid confusion:

```
geosynset-lexicalentry-pos-sense

geowordsenselexicalentry-pos-sense

geoword-lexicalentry
```

For example, `geosynset-lago-n-1` identifies the synset whose list of members contains the sense 1 of the word *lago* (lake). Therefore, the Uniform Resource Identifiers of the resources corresponding to the main classes are obtained by combining the basic namespace (hereafter, `base`):[13]
`www.languagelibrary.eu/owl/geodomainWN/`
with the keyword `instances` and the corresponding class identifiers. For example:

```
base/instances/geosynset-lago-n-1
```

is the URI where the geosynset (identified by geosynset-lago-n-1) is accessible.

### 4.4 GeoDomainWN dataset description

Table 4 gives the number of effective *subject-predicate-object* triples.

Table 4: Files, units and triples

| File | Original Units | Triples |
|---|---|---|
| synset | 657 | 1,971 |
| wordsenseandwords | 657 (wordsenses)<br>632 (words) | 4,781 |

Since the GeodomainWN synsets are 1 : 1 mapped onto the geonames ontology, the final resource also contains 657 relations which connect the concepts using the `owl:sameAs` property.

### 4.5 GeodomainWN in *lemon*

*lemon* (LExicon Model for ONtologies)[14] (McCrae et al., 2011) is a descriptive model that supports the linking up of a computational lexical resource with the semantic information stored in one or more ontologies, as well as enabling the publishing of such lexical resources on the web according to the (L)LOD paradigm.

Following the work performed in the Monnet project[15] for creating a WordNet in *lemon*[16] we decided to transform the GeodomainWN into *lemon*. The resulting resource is a collection of *lemon* lexical entries. *lemon* lexical entries are formally equivalent to the *word* in WordNet but contain more details such as the part of speech and the explicit "narrower/broader" relations among *lemon* senses. In view of 632 units, the resulting resource contains 6,373 triples.

[12] http://www.geonames.org/ontology/.

[13] Actually there are two different namespaces, one for Italian: `base/ita`, and one for English `base/eng`.

[14] http://www.lemon-model.net/.

[15] www.monnet-project.eu/.

[16] http://monnetproject.deri.ie/lemonsource/wordnet.

## 5 Data Distribution

The lexical resources described in this paper are freely available from the *datahub* portal[17] which is synchronized with the *languagelibrary* initiative website.[18]

More specifically, interested people can directly access/download the resources from the following endpoints:

**ItalwordNet** from
http://datahub.io/dataset/iwn

**PAROLE SIMPLE CLIPS** from
http://datahub.io/dataset/simple

**GeodomainWN** from
http://datahub.io/dataset/geodomainwn

## 6 General picture

The figure 4 sums up the connections between the datasets described in this paper and the rest of the (L)LOD cloud.

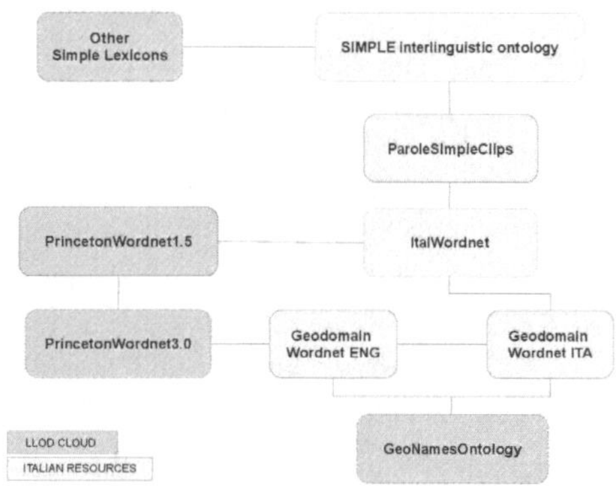


Figure 4: The linguistic linked data network for Italian

The mapping between the PAROLE SIMPLE CLIPS *Usems* and ItalwordNet synsets enriches the synset with semantic information coming from the *Usems*. The depth of information provided by the qualia structure surpasses the one available through (Ital)WordNet, and can be accessed both from Italian and from English, thanks to the IWN - WN$x.y$ mapping.

Although a direct linking between SIMPLE *Usems* in different languages is not currently available, it is imaginable that it might be automatically attempted by combining an automatic translation of the corresponding lexical form and the disambiguation that is provided by the common ontological concepts.

Finally the linking to Geonames connects the presented resources to the non linguistic linked data cloud, for example the word "lago" (lake) is connected to the geonames ontology concept "H.LKS".

## 7 Conclusion and future work

In this paper we have presented three different types of Resource Description Framework (RDF) rendering.

The first one is the conversion of ItalwordNet in RDF according to the rules of the W3C consortium. The second conversion is twofold: a list of domain specific terms has been transformed into a WordNet equivalent resource and then rendered as RDF. This resource has been published also using the *lemon* model (which is the third type of rendering). This exercise will help us to serialize in *lemon* also the complete ItalwordNet resource.

Having mapped the ItalwordNet synsets into the Simple Interlingual Ontology via PSC is fundamental because it provides landscapes for interesting future works and it maps WordNet synsets onto an interesting ontological resource.

Finally the linking to Geonames offers possible applications for Named Entity Recognition and data mining: for example to solve the (Italian) (unambiguous) query such as: "Trova tutti i laghi in Toscana" (Select all lakes in Tuscany), the system uses the "lago" (lake) - H.LKS mapping to perform a query in the Geonames dataset retrieving all instances of that feature concept, namely all lakes, that are located within a specific geographic area, Toscana.

[17] http://www.datahub.io/

[18] http://www.languagelibrary.eu

## References


Núria Bel, Federica Busa, Nicoletta Calzolari, Elisabetta Gola, Alessandro Lenci, Monica Monachini, Antoine Ogonowski, Ivonne Peters, Wim Peters, Nilda Ruimy, Marta Villegas, and Antonio Zampolli. 2000. Simple: A general framework for the development of multilingual lexicons. In *Proceedings of LREC 2000*, Athens, Greece.

Tim Berners-Lee. 2006. Linked data. *W3C Design Issues.*

Christian Chiarcos, Sebastian Hellmann, and Sebastian Nordhoff. 2011. Towards a linguistic linked open data cloud: The open linguistics working group. *TAL*, 52(3):245–275.

Christian Chiarcos. 2012. *Linked Data in Linguistics*. Springer.

Riccardo del Gratta, Francesca Frontini, Fahad Khan, and Monica Monachini. 2013. Converting the parole simple clips lexicon into rdf with lemon. *Semantic Web Journal (Submitted)*.

Christiane Fellbaum. 2010. Wordnet. In Roberto Poli, Michael Healy, and Achilles Kameas, editors, *Theory and Applications of Ontology: Computer Applications*, pages 231–243. Springer Netherlands.

Francesca Frontini, Carlo Aliprandi, Clara Bacciu, Roberto Bartolini, Andrea Marchetti, Enrico Parenti, Fulvio Piccinonno, and Tiziana Soru. 2012. Gloss, an infrastructure for the semantic annotation and mining of documents in the public security domain. In *EEOP2012: Exploring and Exploiting Official Publications Workshop Programme*, page 21.

Ora Lassila and Ralph R. Swick. 1999. Resource description framework (RDF). model and syntax specification. Technical report, W3C, 2.

Alessandro Lenci, Nuria Bel, Federica Busa, Nicoletta Calzolari, Elisabetta Gola, Monica Monachini, Antoine Ogonowski, Ivonne Peters, Wim Peters, Nilda Ruimy, Marta Villegas, and Antonio Zampolli. 2000. Simple: A general framework for the development of multilingual lexicons. *International Journal of Lexicography*, 13(4):249–263.

Leonardo Lezcano, Salvador Sanchez, and Antonio J Roa-Valverde. 2013. A survey on the exchange of linguistic resources: Publishing linguistic linked open data on the web. *Program: electronic library and information systems*, 47(3):3–3.

John McCrae, Dennis Spohr, and Philipp Cimiano. 2011. Linking lexical resources and ontologies on the semantic web with lemon. In *Proceedings of the 8th extended semantic web conference on The semantic web: research and applications - Volume Part I*, ESWC'11, pages 245–259, Berlin, Heidelberg. Springer-Verlag.

James Pustejovsky. 1991. The generative lexicon. *Comput. Linguist.*, 17(4):409–441, dec.

Adriana Roventini, Antonietta Alonge, Francesca Bertagna, Nicoletta Calzolari, Christian Girardi, Bernardo Magnini, Rita Marinelli, and Antonio Zampolli. 2003. Italwordnet: building a large semantic database for the automatic treatment of italian. *Computational Linguistics in Pisa, Special Issue, XVIII-XIX, Pisa-Roma, IEPI*, 2:745–791.

N. Ruimy, O. Corazzari, E. Gola, A. Spanu, N. Calzolari, and A. Zampolli. 1998. The european le-parole project: The italian syntactic lexicon. In *Proceedings of the First International Conference on Language resources and Evaluation*, pages 241–248.

Nilda Ruimy, Monica Monachini, Raffaella Distante, Elisabetta Guazzini, Stefano Molino, Marisa Ulivieri, Nicoletta Calzolari, and Antonio Zampolli. 2002. Clips, a multi-level italian computational lexicon: a glimpse to data. In *Proceedings of LREC 2002*, Las Palmas, Canary Islands, Spain.

Antonio Toral and Monica Monachini. 2007. Simple-owl: a generative lexicon ontology for nlp and the semantic web. In *Workshop of Cooperative Construction of Linguistic Knowledge Bases, 10th Congress of Italian Association for Artificial Intelligence*.

Marta Villegas and Nuria Bel. 2013. Parole/simple lexinfo ontology and lexicons. *Semantic Web Journal (Submitted)*.